SALAD

RECIPES AND TEXT
GEORGEANNE BRENNAN

GENERAL EDITOR
CHUCK WILLIAMS

PHOTOGRAPHS
NOEL BARNHURST

APPLE

CONTENTS

AUTUMN

WINTER

PICNIC SALADS

INTRODUCTION

The essence of a good salad is simplicity. Clean, bright flavors that, when brought together, bring out the best in one another. Part of the art of making a truly superb salad is choosing the freshest ingredients—in particular, vegetables and fruits that have become ripe in their natural season. Although it is easy nowadays to find asparagus in autumn and tomatoes in midwinter, these foods will still taste better in spring and summer. This is why the recipe chapters in this book are arranged primarily by season, to help you find the right salad for the moment. Included is a chapter of classic salads that will never go out of fashion, and a selection of portable picnic salads that can be expanded to feed a crowd.

Each recipe in this cookbook is kitchen-tested and highlights a particular ingredient, term, or technique. A chapter of basics in the back of the book offers an overview of salad making, with all the information you'll need. It is my hope that the recipes in this book will inspire you to get into the kitchen and start cooking!

THE CLASSICS

Certain salads, by virtue of their distinctive combinations of flavor and texture, have earned a place of honor in our collective culinary memory. Over the years, these classics have evolved or given rise to innumerable variations. The recipes that follow represent a return to the original forms of many of our favorite salads, with just a slight adjustment if needed for today's palates.

CAESAR SALAD

PARMESAN CHEESE
True Parmesan comes from
the Emilia-Romagna region of
northern Italy and is referred
to by its trademarked name,
Parmigiano-Reggiano. For
freshness, request a wedge
of Parmesan that has just
been sliced from a wheel.
Rich and complex in flavor
and possessing a pleasant
granular texture, this savory
cheese is excellent shaved
over salads. For shavings,
draw a vegetable peeler
or small knife across a
block of cheese to create
thin sheets and curls.

Preheat the oven to 350°F (180°C). Spread the bread cubes on a baking sheet and sprinkle them with the 3 tablespoons olive oil, ½ teaspoon salt, and ½ teaspoon pepper. Place in the oven and toast, turning once or twice, until golden, about 15 minutes. Remove the cubes from the sheet, let cool, and rub one or two sides of each cube with the unpeeled garlic. (The rough edges of the toast act as a grater.) Set aside.

In the bottom of a salad bowl, using a fork, crush the peeled garlic with ½ teaspoon salt to make a paste. Crush 4 anchovy fillets into the paste. Whisk in the Worcestershire sauce, vinegar, and ½ teaspoon pepper. While whisking, slowly drizzle in the remaining ⅓ cup olive oil to make a thick dressing.

Add the lettuce leaves and three-fourths of the croutons to the bowl with the dressing and mix gently but well. Break the egg into the bowl and mix again. Top with the remaining croutons. Scatter the Parmesan shavings over the salad and serve at once, garnished with anchovy fillets, if desired.

Note: This dish contains raw egg. If desired, omit the egg. For more information, see page 114.

MAKES 4 SERVINGS

2 cups (4 oz/125 g) cubed sourdough or other coarse country bread (1-inch/2.5-cm cubes)

3 tablespoons plus ⅓ cup (3 fl oz/80 ml) extra-virgin olive oil

Salt and freshly ground pepper

6 cloves garlic, 3 unpeeled and 3 peeled

4 anchovy fillets, plus extra for optional garnish

1 teaspoon Worcestershire sauce

2 teaspoons red wine vinegar

2 hearts romaine (cos) lettuce, separated into leaves

1 egg

Parmesan cheese shavings for garnish *(far left)*

COBB SALAD

3 peeled hard-boiled eggs
(far right)

8 slices bacon

1 head romaine (cos) lettuce,
leaves separated and torn
into bite-sized pieces

2 tablespoons minced fresh
flat-leaf (Italian) parsley

2 tablespoons minced fresh
chives, plus several longer
chive lengths

2 cups (4 oz/125 g)
chopped watercress
(tough stems removed)

4 cups (1½ lb/750 g) diced
cooked turkey or chicken
(see Note)

2 avocados, pitted, peeled,
and diced

2 tomatoes, chopped

¼ lb (125 g) plus 1 oz (30 g)
Roquefort cheese, crumbled

¼ cup (2 fl oz/60 ml)
red wine vinegar

1 teaspoon Worcestershire
sauce

½ teaspoon Dijon mustard

1 clove garlic, crushed and
then minced

Salt and ground pepper

⅓ cup (3 fl oz/80 ml)
extra-virgin olive oil

Cut the hard-boiled eggs into ½-inch (12-mm) dice. Set aside.

In a frying pan over medium heat, fry the bacon until crisp, about 10 minutes. Transfer to paper towels to drain. When cool, crumble and set aside.

Make a bed of lettuce on a platter or shallow bowl. Mix together the parsley and minced chives. Arrange the eggs, bacon, mixed minced herbs, watercress, turkey, avocados, tomatoes, and the ¼ lb cheese in a neat pattern atop the bed of romaine, in rows or in a checkerboard pattern, covering the lettuce almost completely.

In a small bowl, whisk together the vinegar, Worcestershire sauce, mustard, garlic, ¼ teaspoon salt, and ½ teaspoon pepper. Using a fork, mash in the remaining 1 oz cheese to make a paste. While whisking, slowly drizzle in the olive oil to form a thick dressing.

Pour a little of the dressing over the salad and garnish with chive lengths. Serve at once. Pass the remaining dressing at the table.

Note: For the cooked poultry in this recipe, use leftover roasted turkey or chicken. If you have none on hand, poach some chicken breasts. Put 4 or 5 bone-in chicken breast halves in a large saucepan and add lightly salted water to cover. Bring to a boil over high heat. Reduce the heat to low and simmer for 30 minutes. Remove from the heat and let stand for 30 minutes. Discard the skin and bones and cut the meat into bite-sized pieces.

Variation Tip: Traditionally, this salad is made with Roquefort cheese, which gives a richness and tang to the dressing as well as to the salad. Some may prefer a milder blue cheese, however, such as Danish or Maytag.

MAKES 4–6 SERVINGS

HARD-BOILED EGGS

It's easy to overcook hard-boiled eggs, giving their yolks an unsightly greenish tinge and a dry texture. This gentle method ensures good results: Put the eggs in a saucepan and add cold water to cover them by 2 inches (5 cm). Bring to a boil over medium heat. When the water begins to boil, remove from the heat, cover, and let the eggs stand in the water for 20 minutes. Rinse under cold running water until cool, then peel.

POTATO SALAD

POTATO TYPES

The role of potatoes in a dish determines the type of potato that should be used. Waxy potatoes, called for here, hold their shape during boiling or steaming and are used in dishes that call for potato slices or cubes. Starchy potatoes, like the russet or baking potato, break down when cooked, which is more desirable for baked or mashed potatoes.

Cut the hard-boiled eggs into slices ¼ inch (6 mm) thick. Set aside.

In a large saucepan, combine the potatoes, 2 teaspoons salt, and water to cover by 2 inches (5 cm). Bring to a boil over medium-high heat, reduce the heat to medium, and cook, uncovered, until the potatoes are tender and can be easily pierced with a fork, 20–25 minutes. Drain and, when just cool enough to handle, peel and cut into ½-inch (12-mm) cubes. Place the still-warm potatoes in a large bowl.

In a small bowl, stir together the mayonnaise, sour cream, pickle juice, and mustard to taste. Spoon this over the potatoes and mix gently but thoroughly. Add the onion, fresh dill, pickle, celery, 1 teaspoon salt, and ½ teaspoon pepper. Again, mix gently but thoroughly. Taste and adjust the seasoning. Add all but 5 of the egg slices, mixing them gently into the salad.

Transfer the salad to a serving bowl and garnish with the reserved egg slices and a sprinkle of paprika. Cover and refrigerate for at least 1 hour or up to 24 hours before serving.

To serve as an attractive first course, line small plates with lettuce leaves, then top with a mound of the salad.

Variation Tip: Other ingredients can be added to potato salad, such as diced cooked shrimp, flaked canned tuna, coarsely chopped olives, or chopped or slivered pimientos. For a warm potato salad with vinegar, see page 65.

MAKES 4–6 SERVINGS

5 peeled hard-boiled eggs (page 13)

2½ lb (1.25 kg) small waxy potatoes such as Yukon gold, Yellow Finn, or Red Rose

Salt and freshly ground pepper

½ cup (4 fl oz/125 ml) mayonnaise, preferably homemade (page 111)

½ cup (4 oz/125 g) light sour cream

1 tablespoon sweet pickle juice

1–2 tablespoons Dijon mustard

¾ cup (4 oz/125 g) minced red onion

½ cup (¾ oz/20 g) chopped fresh dill

¼ cup (1½ oz/45 g) minced sweet pickle

½ cup (2½ oz/75 g) chopped celery

1 teaspoon sweet paprika

Lettuce leaves for serving (optional)

SALADE NIÇOISE

4 peeled hard-boiled eggs (page 13)

1 lb (500 g) small waxy potatoes such as Yukon gold, Yellow Finn, or Red Rose

Salt and freshly ground pepper

1 lb (500 g) slender green beans such as haricots verts or baby Blue Lakes, trimmed

2 cups (1½ oz/45 g) mixed young salad greens

16 anchovy fillets

5 tomatoes, thinly sliced

1 green bell pepper (capsicum), seeded and cut lengthwise into narrow strips

½ cup (2½ oz/75 g) oil-cured black olives

1 can (8 oz/250 g) olive oil–packed tuna, drained

¼ cup (2 fl oz/60 ml) red wine vinegar

2 tablespoons minced shallot

¼ cup (2 fl oz/60 ml) extra-virgin olive oil

Quarter the hard-boiled eggs lengthwise. Set aside.

Put the potatoes and ¾ teaspoon salt in a large saucepan and add water to cover by 2 inches (5 cm). Bring to a boil over medium-high heat, reduce the heat to medium, and cook, uncovered, until the potatoes are tender and can be pierced easily with a fork, 20–25 minutes. Drain, rinse with cold running water, and, when just cool enough to handle, peel and cut into slices about ¼ inch (6 mm) thick. Set aside.

Arrange the beans in a steamer basket and place over boiling water. Cover and steam just until tender, about 3 minutes. Lift out the basket and place under cold running water to stop the cooking. Drain and set aside.

Divide the salad greens among individual plates, making a bed on each. Divide the ingredients evenly, arranging the eggs, potatoes, beans, anchovy fillets, tomatoes, bell pepper, and olives on each plate, with the tuna in the center.

In a small bowl, whisk together the vinegar, shallot, ½ teaspoon salt, and ½ teaspoon pepper. While whisking, slowly drizzle in the olive oil to make a thick dressing. Pour the dressing over the salads and serve at once.

Variation Tip: Additional ingredients, such as peeled and sliced cucumber, shredded carrots, and diced cooked beets, are sometimes included in a Niçoise salad as well.

MAKES 6 SERVINGS

NIÇOISE TRADITION

This classic salad of Nice, in southern France, was originally made with canned, not fresh, tuna, although of late it has become fashionable (especially in restaurants in the United States) to use grilled fresh tuna instead. Many traditionalists claim that not only must the tuna be canned, but also the vegetables must be raw, never cooked. When ordering the salad in a restaurant today, however, you will find some cooked vegetables and some raw, as in this version.

CELERY ROOT RÉMOULADE

In a saucepan, combine the celery root, 1 teaspoon salt, lemon juice, and water to cover by about 2 inches (5 cm). Bring to a boil over medium-high heat and cook for 3–4 minutes. The celery root should be just tender to the bite, not mushy. Drain well and, using a sharp knife, slice into thinner rounds, then cut into very thin strips. Alternatively, stack the slices and use a mandoline to shred them. Place in a bowl.

In a small bowl, stir together the mayonnaise and 2 tablespoons of the mustard. Taste the mixture. It should be well seasoned with the mustard but still taste of both ingredients. Add more mustard as desired. Pour the dressing over the celery root and mix well. Cover and refrigerate for at least 1 hour or up to 12 hours before serving. Serve mounded on a salad plate or in a bowl.

1 large or 2 medium celery roots (celeriacs), peeled and cut into rounds ¼ inch (6 mm) thick *(far left)*

Salt

2 tablespoons fresh lemon juice

1 cup (8 fl oz/250 ml) mayonnaise, preferably homemade (page 111)

2–3 tablespoons Dijon mustard

Note: In traditional French bistros, celery root rémoulade is served as part of an assortment of small, individual vegetable salads, such as diced beets, cubed potatoes, grated carrots, or sliced tomatoes, all dressed with vinaigrette. The most traditional version of the recipe calls for raw celery root sliced paper-thin and then julienned. The vegetable is briefly cooked in this version to make it more tender.

Serving Tip: To serve as an elegant first course, make a bed of baby spinach, watercress, or red-leaf lettuce on individual salad plates and spoon the salad onto the center.

MAKES 4 SERVINGS

PREPARING CELERY ROOT

Also called celeriac, celery root has a much stronger, more pungent flavor than its better-known relative, head celery. It has a tough, dark brown skin covered with fine, hairlike roots and larger, fleshy roots at the base. To remove the skin, use a sharp knife, peeling it much as you would the skin of an apple. Also like an apple, the flesh of celery root discolors upon exposure to air. Once peeled, it should be immersed in water to which a little lemon juice or vinegar has been added, unless it is to be used immediately.

INSALATA CAPRESE

8 ripe tomatoes, sliced

1 lb (500 g) fresh
mozzarella cheese,
thinly sliced

½ cup (½ oz/15 g) fresh
basil leaves

¼ cup (2 fl oz/60 ml)
extra-virgin olive oil

Salt, preferably sea salt,
and freshly ground pepper

On a platter, alternate slices of tomato and mozzarella. Garnish generously with basil leaves, tucking some underneath the tomatoes. Drizzle the olive oil over all, and then sprinkle with ½ teaspoon each salt and pepper. Serve at once.

Note: Some recipes for insalata caprese *add other herbs and even capers, but the purest version relies on just four perfect ingredients: vine-ripened tomatoes, fresh mozzarella, bright green basil, and fruity olive oil. Use only the very ripest tomatoes, as their juices mix with the olive oil to make the dressing. It is important that the oil be of the highest quality, because the difference between an average olive oil and a superior one will be evident here.*

Serving Tip: This salad may also be arranged as an antipasto, or appetizer. Using small plum (Roma) tomatoes, top each tomato slice with a slice of fresh mozzarella and a basil leaf.

MAKES 4–6 SERVINGS

FRESH MOZZARELLA

This classic salad from the island of Capri, just off Italy's southern coast near Naples, is made with fresh mozzarella, one of the country's best-known cheeses. Soft and spongy textured, it is sold packed in liquid at well-stocked supermarkets, cheese stores, and Italian groceries. Fresh mozzarella was traditionally made from the milk of the water buffalo, but cow's milk is used else-where and increasingly in Italy, as well.

AMBROSIA

PREPARING PINEAPPLE

To peel and core a pineapple, first cut off the crown of leaves and the bottom end. Set the pineapple straight up on one end and pare off the skin, cutting downward just below the surface in long, vertical strips and leaving the small brown eyes on the fruit. Place the pineapple on its side. Aligning the knife's blade with the diagonal rows of eyes, cut shallow furrows, following a spiral pattern, to remove all the eyes. Cut the pineapple crosswise into round slices ½ inch (12 mm) thick and remove the fibrous center core with a knife or small cookie cutter.

Cut the pineapple slices into ½-inch (12-mm) cubes, capturing as much of the juice as possible. Place the cubes and juice in a bowl.

Cut a slice off the top and bottom of 1 orange, then stand it upright. Following the contour of the fruit, slice off the peel and white pith in thick strips. Holding the fruit over a bowl, carefully cut along each side of the membranes between the sections, letting each freed section and any juices drop into the bowl. Cut each section in half crosswise, again capturing as much of the juice as possible and returning them to the bowl. Repeat with the remaining 4 oranges.

Add the banana slices to the bowl, and sprinkle the lemon juice and the Cointreau, if using, over the fruit. Scatter the coconut and grapes over the top and mix gently but thoroughly. Cover and refrigerate for at least 1 hour or up to 12 hours before serving.

Transfer to a serving bowl or individual bowls and serve chilled.

Variation Tip: Sometimes miniature marshmallows are added to ambrosia, as are maraschino cherries. If you add marshmallows, gently mix them into the salad just before serving. If you add cherries, use them as a last-minute topping or garnish, as they will stain the other fruit and the coconut if added sooner.

MAKES 6–8 SERVINGS

½ pineapple, peeled, sliced crosswise, and cored
(far left)

5 navel oranges

3 bananas, peeled and cut into slices a generous ¼ inch (6 mm) thick

1 tablespoon fresh lemon juice

2 teaspoons Cointreau or other orange-flavored liqueur (optional)

½ cup (2 oz/60 g) sweetened shredded dried coconut

1 cup (6 oz/185 g) seedless grapes, green, red, or a mixture

22

SPRING

Spring is the season of tender new growth after winter's sleep. Leaves are dainty and delicate, pods sweet and succulent. During these months, light salads that utilize the sprightly flavors of fresh seasonal ingredients are tempting and easy to make. Dressings should be equally restrained, incorporating herbs, citrus, and ginger, and allowing the tastes of the season to shine.

GREEN HERB SALAD
WITH CHAMPAGNE VINAIGRETTE
26

ASPARAGUS AND SMOKED SALMON
WITH TARRAGON CREAM
29

FAVAS, GREEN BEANS, PEAS,
AND ZUCCHINI RIBBONS
30

CHICKEN, AVOCADO, AND MANGO SALAD
33

BABY SPINACH WITH
GINGER-GLAZED SCALLOPS
34

ARTICHOKES WITH
BREAD-AND-TOMATO STUFFING
37

SPRING LETTUCES WITH
BROILED GOAT CHEESE
38

GREEN HERB SALAD
WITH CHAMPAGNE VINAIGRETTE

In the bottom of a salad bowl, combine the olive oil and the shallot. Add the vinegar, ¼ teaspoon salt, and ¼ teaspoon pepper and mix well with a fork. Top with the lettuce, parsley, cilantro, and chervil.

When ready to serve, toss well. Mound the salad in individual serving bowls or on plates.

Make-Ahead Tip: Before tossing, the dressing and salad can stand for up to 30 minutes.

Variation Tip: To enrich the dressing, add a little Maytag, Stilton, Gorgonzola, or other blue-veined cheese along with the vinegar, coarsely mashing it with a fork. Serve the salad accompanied with a sliver of the cheese and some walnuts after a main course.

MAKES 4 SERVINGS

HERB SALADS

In many Mediterranean countries, fresh herbs are used as primary salad ingredients. Herbs are appreciated for the complex flavor and refreshing taste they bring to a salad. Parsley, cilantro (fresh coriander), chervil, arugula (rocket), and mint are commonly used this way. Fresh oregano and thyme might be used in smaller quantities. You may use only a single herb or a mixture. Do not use woody-stemmed herbs such as rosemary or sage.

¼ cup (2 fl oz/60 ml) extra-virgin olive oil

1 tablespoon minced shallot

2 tablespoons Champagne vinegar

Salt and freshly ground pepper

1 large head butter (Boston) lettuce, leaves separated and torn into bite-sized pieces

1 cup (1 oz/30 g) fresh flat-leaf (Italian) parsley leaves

½ cup (½ oz/15 g) fresh cilantro (fresh coriander) leaves

½ cup (½ oz/15 g) fresh chervil sprigs

ASPARAGUS AND SMOKED SALMON WITH TARRAGON CREAM

FOR THE TARRAGON CREAM:

1 cup (8 fl oz/250 ml) heavy (double) cream

2 tablespoons cider vinegar

1 teaspoon fresh lemon juice

Salt and freshly ground pepper

2 tablespoons minced fresh tarragon

1½ lb (750 g) asparagus, trimmed (far right)

⅓ lb (5 oz/155 g) smoked salmon, thinly sliced

1½ teaspoons fresh lemon juice

Fresh tarragon sprigs for garnish

To make the tarragon cream, put the cream in a small bowl, then whisk in the cider vinegar, 1 teaspoon lemon juice, ¼ teaspoon salt, ¼ teaspoon pepper, and the tarragon. Set aside. The cream will curdle and thicken within 4–5 minutes.

Arrange the asparagus in a steamer basket and place over boiling water. Cover and steam until just tender to the bite, 3–4 minutes. Transfer the asparagus to a colander and immediately place under cold running water to stop the cooking and to preserve the bright green color. Slice the spears on the diagonal about ½ inch (12 mm) thick, leaving some whole if desired. Set aside.

Arrange the salmon on a platter or individual plates. Drizzle evenly with the 1½ teaspoons lemon juice. Top with the asparagus, garnish with the tarragon sprigs, and serve with the tarragon cream.

Make-Ahead Tip: The tarragon cream and asparagus may be chilled before serving.

Variation Tips: The tarragon cream is also excellent spooned over room-temperature green beans or sliced tomatoes. Or, other delicate green herbs such as chervil, dill, or parsley can be substituted for the tarragon.

MAKES 4 SERVINGS

TRIMMING ASPARAGUS

To ensure the best flavor and texture for asparagus, bend the cut end of each spear until it breaks naturally. It will snap precisely where the fibrous inedible portion begins. To give all the spears a consistent length, trim them with a knife after you have snapped off the ends. If the spears have a thick or fibrous skin (check by taking a small bite), peel them to within about 1 inch (2.5 cm) of the tips.

FAVAS, GREEN BEANS, PEAS, AND ZUCCHINI RIBBONS

Bring a large saucepan three-fourths full of water to a boil over medium-high heat and add ½ teaspoon salt and the fava beans. Boil until just tender, about 6 minutes. Do not overcook. Drain and rinse with cold water to stop the cooking. Drain again, then skin each fava bean *(left)*. Set aside.

Meanwhile, bring a smaller saucepan three-fourths full of water to a boil over medium-high heat and add ¼ teaspoon salt and the peas. Boil until just tender, 3–5 minutes. As with the favas, do not overcook. Drain and rinse with cold water to stop the cooking. Drain again and set aside.

Arrange the green beans in a steamer basket and place over boiling water. Cover and steam just until tender, about 3 minutes. Lift out the basket and rinse with cold water to stop the cooking. Drain and set aside.

Using a vegetable peeler, peel the zucchini. Then, still using the vegetable peeler, cut the flesh of the zucchini into long, thin fettuccine-like ribbons. Set aside.

In a bowl, combine the garlic and ½ teaspoon salt. Using a fork, crush them into a paste. Still using the fork, mix in the olive oil, then the lemon juice and ½ teaspoon pepper. Pour this mixture into a large bowl and add the favas, peas, green beans, zucchini ribbons, and basil. Mix until well coated, cover, and refrigerate for at least 1½ hours or up to 5 hours.

To serve, gently mix all but 4 or 5 of the anchovy fillets into the vegetables. Transfer the mixture to a serving bowl or a platter and top with the remaining anchovies. Scatter the Parmesan shavings over all. Serve at once.

MAKES 4 SERVINGS

PREPARING FAVA BEANS

Before cooking, fresh fava beans must first be shelled, or removed from their pods. Unless they have been picked while still quite young and small, the skin that covers each shelled bean is thick and tough, and the beans must be skinned before eating. To remove the skins, drop the shelled beans into boiling water, drain, and let cool. Using a small knife, pierce the skin of each bean opposite the end where it was attached to the pod and squeeze lightly. The bean will pop free of its skin.

Salt and freshly ground pepper

2 lb (1 kg) fava (broad) beans, shelled

1 lb (500 g) English peas, shelled

½ lb (250 g) slender green beans such as haricots verts or baby Blue Lakes, trimmed

4 zucchini (courgettes), about 1 lb (500 g) total weight

2 cloves garlic

⅓ cup (3 fl oz/80 ml) extra-virgin olive oil

3 tablespoons fresh lemon juice

⅓ cup (½ oz/15 g) julienned fresh basil leaves

15 anchovy fillets

½ cup (2 oz/60 g) Parmesan cheese shavings

CHICKEN, AVOCADO, AND MANGO SALAD

3 bone-in chicken breast
halves, about 2 lb (1 kg)
total weight

Salt and freshly ground
pepper

5 tablespoons (3 fl oz/
80 ml) fresh lime juice

1 tablespoon peeled and
minced fresh ginger

2 teaspoons grapeseed
or other light oil

3 tablespoons minced
fresh cilantro (fresh coriander), plus 1 cup (1 oz/30 g)
whole leaves

4–5 rounded cups (about
6 oz/185 g) torn lettuce
leaves such as red leaf,
green leaf, or oak leaf, or a
mixture (bite-sized pieces)

3 mangoes, peeled
and sliced

2 avocados, pitted, peeled,
and sliced

2 tablespoons minced
red onion, plus several
thin slices

Preheat the oven to 350°F (180°C). Rub the chicken breasts with
½ teaspoon salt and ½ teaspoon pepper and place, skin side up,
on a baking sheet. Roast until the skin is crisp and the meat is
cooked through but still moist, 40–50 minutes. Remove from the
oven and let stand until cool enough to handle, then remove the
skin and discard. Cut the chicken meat from the bones and into
bite-sized pieces, then set aside.

In the bottom of a large bowl, whisk together 2 tablespoons of the
lime juice, the ginger, ¼ teaspoon salt, the oil, and 1 tablespoon
of the minced cilantro. Add the 1 cup whole cilantro leaves and
the lettuce and mix well with the dressing.

Arrange the dressed greens on a platter and evenly distribute the
mango slices over the top. Drizzle with 1 tablespoon of the lime
juice. Arrange the chicken over the top, and then the avocado
slices. Drizzle the avocado with the remaining 2 tablespoons lime
juice. Sprinkle the remaining 2 tablespoons minced cilantro and
the red onion over the top. Serve immediately.

*Make-Ahead Tip: The chicken can be cooked, cooled, and cut into
pieces up to 1 day in advance of serving. Cover and refrigerate, then
bring to room temperature before combining with the other salad
ingredients.*

*Variation Tip: To make a breakfast version of this salad, use sliced
cantaloupe in place of the chicken, and serve the salad accompanied
with toast spread with tropical fruit jams.*

MAKES 4 OR 5 SERVINGS

CHOOSING LIMES

The lime is a close cousin of
the lemon, but with a sweeter
taste that especially heightens
the flavor of other fruits,
including melons, nectarines,
peaches, and plums, as well
as the mango and avocado
used here. The two most
well-known lime varieties are
the common green Persian
lime and the slightly smaller,
tart Key lime, also called the
Mexican lime. Either will
work for this recipe. Limes
are ripe when they give
slightly to pressure and when
the rind releases a sharp,
aromatic scent if scraped
with a fingernail.

BABY SPINACH WITH
GINGER-GLAZED SCALLOPS

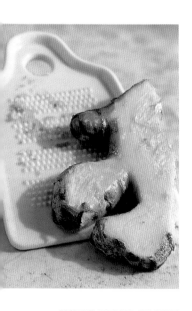

USING FRESH GINGER

Look for fresh ginger that feels heavy in the hand and shows no wrinkling or other signs of age. To prepare it, use a vegetable peeler or paring knife to remove the thin beige skin. Once peeled, it is often grated to capture its flavor without its fibrous texture. Porcelain ginger graters, specially designed to let you use the aromatic juice and flesh without the tough fibers, are sold in Asian markets and specialty cookware stores. Or, use the small rasps on a metal grater.

In a small nonaluminum saucepan, combine the minced shallot and the grapefruit juice and let stand for about 10 minutes. Add the lime and lemon juices and place the pan over medium-high heat. Bring to a boil and cook until the liquid has reduced slightly to about ½ cup (4 fl oz/125 ml), 1–2 minutes. Remove from the heat and stir in 1½ teaspoons of the oil and ¼ teaspoon salt. Set the dressing aside.

In a small bowl or cup, stir together the soy sauce, ginger, honey, and mustard to make a glaze and set aside.

Just before beginning to cook the scallops, put the spinach in a bowl and pour the dressing over it. Toss well. Divide the dressed spinach among individual salad plates.

In a frying pan large enough to hold all the scallops in a single layer without crowding, warm the remaining 2½ teaspoons oil over medium-high heat. When it is hot, add the scallops and sear, turning once, until golden, about 30 seconds on each side. Add the soy sauce mixture, reduce the heat to low, and turn the scallops in the sauce for about 45 seconds. They will be glazed a deep mahogany brown.

Divide the scallops among the plates, placing them atop the spinach. Drizzle with any sauce remaining in the pan. Serve immediately.

Serving Tip: Grapefruit and scallops are excellent partners. Play up this affinity by adding a few segments of carefully peeled grapefruit to each plate. Garnish with grapefruit zest or lime slices.

MAKES 4 SERVINGS

1 tablespoon minced shallot

½ cup (4 fl oz/125 ml) fresh grapefruit juice

1½ tablespoons fresh lime juice

1½ teaspoons fresh lemon juice

4 teaspoons grapeseed, canola, or other light oil

Salt

2½ tablespoons soy sauce

1½ tablespoons peeled and grated fresh ginger *(far left)*

1½ teaspoons honey

½ teaspoon Dijon mustard

¾ lb (375 g) baby spinach leaves

8 sea scallops, about ½ lb (250 g) total weight

ARTICHOKES WITH
BREAD-AND-TOMATO STUFFING

4 medium to large
artichokes, trimmed
(far right)

4 cups (8 oz/250 g) torn
day-old coarse country
bread

About ½ cup (4 fl oz/
125 ml) red wine vinegar,
or to taste

About ¼ cup (2 fl oz/
60 ml) water

¼ cup (2 fl oz/60 ml)
olive oil, or to taste

4 tomatoes, peeled and
seeded (page 115), then
finely chopped

1 cup (1½ oz/45 g) minced
fresh flat-leaf (Italian)
parsley, plus sprigs for
garnish

½ cup (4 oz/125 g) capers,
rinsed and chopped

Salt and freshly ground
pepper

Place the artichokes on a steamer rack over boiling water, cover, and steam until a fork easily pierces the base of an artichoke, 30–40 minutes. Remove from the pan and set upside down to drain and cool.

Meanwhile, put the bread in a bowl and add half of the vinegar and half of the water. Let soak, turning occasionally, until the bread absorbs the liquid to the extent that it crumbles easily between your fingertips. The drier and coarser the bread, the more liquid you will need, so add as much of the remaining vinegar and water as necessary. When enough liquid has been absorbed, crumble the bread into soft crumbs. Add the ¼ cup olive oil, tomatoes, minced parsley, capers, 1 teaspoon salt, and ½ teaspoon pepper and mix well. The stuffing should be quite moist. If necessary, add a little more oil, vinegar, or other seasonings to your taste.

To prepare each artichoke for stuffing, gently spread the inner leaves apart. Using a metal spoon, scoop out the small, pale inner leaves and the hairy choke to create a cavity. Fill the cavity with some of the stuffing, mounding it slightly. Now, gently separate the outer leaves and, using a teaspoon and your fingertips, tuck in a little stuffing at the base of each row of leaves. Set the artichoke on a platter and repeat with the remaining artichokes.

Cover the platter with plastic wrap and refrigerate the artichokes for at least 4 hours or up to 12 hours before serving. Transfer to individual plates and serve chilled, garnished with parsley sprigs.

MAKES 4 SERVINGS

TRIMMING
ARTICHOKES

As you trim artichokes, use acidulated water to keep their cut surfaces from turning gray upon exposure to air. Add the juice of 1 lemon to a large bowl of water. Snap off any tough outer leaves from each artichoke and trim the stem even with the base. Cut off the top third of the leaves with a serrated knife, and trim away any remaining thorns with kitchen scissors. As you finish trimming each artichoke, drop it into the bowl of acidulated water to slow its discoloration.

SPRING LETTUCES WITH BROILED GOAT CHEESE

Preheat the broiler (grill). Line a broiler pan with aluminum foil.

Divide the cheese into 4 equal portions and shape each portion into a patty a scant ½ inch (12 mm) thick. Place the patties on the foil-lined pan and set aside.

In a salad bowl, whisk together the vinegar, ¼ teaspoon salt, and ½ teaspoon pepper. While whisking, slowly drizzle in the olive oil to make a thick dressing. Add the greens and toss to coat well. Divide among individual plates and set aside.

Broil (grill) the goat cheese patties about 8 inches (20 cm) from the heat source until the cheese is just heated through and has softened along the bottom edge, about 4 minutes.

Remove the pan from the broiler and place a patty atop each salad. Give a final sprinkling of pepper and serve immediately.

Note: Warm goat cheese salads are a staple in France, where they are often served atop a thin slice of toasted baguette, accompanied with a few more toasts. In another version, the dressed salad leaves are topped with a poached egg and the warm goat cheese and the toasts are served alongside.

MAKES 4 SERVINGS

GOAT CHEESE STYLES

Goat cheese, a longtime specialty of French cheese makers, is sold in a range of styles, from only a few days old and quite soft to months old and very dry. As the cheese ages, its flavor becomes more pungent and pronounced. Soft fresh goat cheeses are sold in *tommes*—small to medium rounds—or shaped into pyramids, balls, or logs. They may be seasoned with herbs, pepper, or nuts, or they may be rolled in ashes. Hard-aged goat cheese usually comes in the form of a *tomme*.

5 oz (155 g) fresh goat cheese

1½ tablespoons red wine vinegar

Salt and freshly ground pepper

3 tablespoons extra-virgin olive oil

8–10 oz (250–315 g) mixed young salad greens

SUMMER

Summertime salads are assembled from a bounty of colorful vegetables and fruits whose rich flavors have intensified under the steady heat of the sun. Requiring little cooking, hot-weather salads can be as simple as perfectly ripe vegetables, sliced and dressed with a fruity olive oil and a splash of sweet balsamic vinegar, with a few olives or capers providing a tart counterpoint.

GREEK SALAD
WITH CHERRY TOMATOES
42

TABBOULEH
45

TOMATO AND BREAD SALAD
WITH DEEP-FRIED CHICKEN BITES
46

SLENDER GREEN BEANS IN PESTO
49

CORN AND TOMATO SALSA ON
CRISPY CORN TORTILLAS
50

THAI-STYLE GRILLED BEEF SALAD
53

NECTARINE, MELON, AND BLACKBERRY
SALAD WITH FRESH MINT
54

GREEK SALAD
WITH CHERRY TOMATOES

Seed the bell peppers and cut them into 1-inch (2.5-cm) chunks. Stem the cherry tomatoes and halve one-half of them, leaving the others whole. Peel and thickly slice the cucumbers, and thinly slice the red onions. Cut the feta into 1-inch (2.5-cm) cubes. Crush and mince the garlic clove.

In a large bowl, combine the bell peppers, tomatoes, cucumbers, onions, feta cheese, olives, anchovies (if using), and capers and toss together.

In a small bowl, whisk together the vinegar, garlic, dill, oregano, ½ teaspoon salt, and ½ teaspoon pepper. While whisking, slowly drizzle in the olive oil to make a thick dressing. Pour the dressing over the salad, toss, and serve.

Variation Tips: For a more formal presentation, arrange the bell peppers, tomatoes, cucumbers, onions, feta cheese, olives, and anchovies (if using) on a platter. Sprinkle the capers over all the ingredients and pour the dressing over the top. Or, try sliced large tomatoes instead of cherry tomatoes. Line the platter with lettuce leaves or young spinach leaves to make a bed for the other ingredients.

MAKES 8 SERVINGS

CHOOSING OLIVE OIL

The Mediterranean countries are all olive-oil producers, and each country, even each region within a country, has its own style of oil. Oils from Greece tend to be rich, yet mellow. Tuscan oils are distinctly peppery, while Sicilian oils are "big" and earthy. Olive oils from the south coast of France are buttery. Whenever possible, choose oils that match the style of a dish, with lighter, milder oils for delicate salads, vegetables, or fish. More robust olive oils pair well with sturdier vegetables, anchovies, garlic, dark greens, and red meats.

2 red bell peppers (capsicums)

1 green bell pepper (capsicum)

2 cups (12 oz/375 g) cherry tomatoes

2 cucumbers

2 red onions

½ lb (250 g) feta cheese

1 clove garlic

¾ cup (4 oz/125 g) Kalamata olives

6 anchovy fillets (optional)

2 tablespoons capers, rinsed

¼ cup (2 fl oz/60 ml) red wine vinegar

2 tablespoons minced fresh dill

1 teaspoon dried oregano

Salt and freshly ground pepper

⅓ cup (3 fl oz/80 ml) fruity extra-virgin olive oil

TABBOULEH

2 cups (16 fl oz/500 ml) water

Salt and freshly ground pepper

8 teaspoons extra-virgin olive oil

1²/₃ cups (10 oz/315 g) bulgur

¼ cup (2 fl oz/60 ml) fresh lemon juice

1 cup (1½ oz/45 g) chopped fresh mint

1 cup (1½ oz/45 g) chopped fresh flat-leaf (Italian) parsley

2 tomatoes, seeded and diced

1 cucumber, peeled, seeded, and minced

¼ cup (1 oz/30 g) chopped red onion

In a saucepan over high heat, combine the water, ½ teaspoon salt, and 4 teaspoons of the olive oil and bring to a boil. Put the bulgur in a heatproof bowl and pour the boiling mixture over it. Let stand, uncovered, until tender, about 1 hour.

In a large bowl, whisk together the remaining 4 teaspoons olive oil, the lemon juice, ½ teaspoon salt, and ½ teaspoon pepper. Add the bulgur and mix well to coat thoroughly. Now add the mint, parsley, tomatoes, cucumber, and onion and mix well again.

Cover and refrigerate for 2 hours to let the flavors blend. Serve chilled.

Serving Tip: For a festive presentation, fill scooped-out tomato halves with the tabbouleh and place them on lettuce leaves. Garnish with oil-cured black olives.

MAKES 6–8 SERVINGS

GRAIN SALADS

Salads, such as this traditional Lebanese one featuring bulgur, may be based on a wide variety of grains, including *(above, clockwise from left)* barley, bulgur, or millet. Once cooked and cooled, their mild flavor and firm texture make them good vehicles for other flavors, such as dressings made with citrus juices, vinegars, soy sauce, and olive, nut, or seed oils. Virtually any vegetable or fruit may be used in grain salads, and meat or fish can be added, too. Light yet filling, these salads are the perfect supper for a hot summer night.

TOMATO AND BREAD SALAD
WITH DEEP-FRIED CHICKEN BITES

DRIED BREAD CUBES

To make dried bread cubes, cut leftover coarse bread or baguette into 1-inch (2.5-cm) cubes before it dries out. (If it has already dried, it will break into irregular pieces when you try to cut it.) Let the cubes sit out for another day or two. To make dried bread crumbs, let any bread a few days past its peak of freshness dry out in a 200°F (95°C) oven for about 1 hour. Break the bread into bite-sized pieces and then process the pieces in a blender or food processor into fine crumbs.

Preheat the oven to 400°F (200°C). Spread the bread cubes on a baking sheet and drizzle with 2 tablespoons of the olive oil. Bake, turning once, until lightly golden, about 15 minutes. Remove from the pan, let cool, and rub with the 2 unpeeled garlic cloves. Set aside.

In a large bowl, combine the tomatoes, minced garlic, the remaining 3 tablespoons olive oil, vinegar, ½ teaspoon salt, and ½ teaspoon pepper. Mix well.

To prepare the chicken bites, spread the bread crumbs on waxed paper or a plate. Roll the chicken pieces, a few at a time, in the bread crumbs to coat evenly, then set aside.

Pour vegetable oil into a deep frying pan to a depth of 2 inches (5 cm) and heat it until it registers 375°F (190°C) on a deep-frying thermometer. When the oil is hot, add the chicken pieces and fry, turning them as needed, until golden and opaque throughout, about 4 minutes total. Using a slotted spoon, transfer to paper towels to drain briefly.

Add the hot chicken bites, bread cubes, and basil to the tomatoes and mix to distribute all the ingredients evenly. Serve immediately.

MAKES 4 OR 5 SERVINGS

3 cups (6 oz/185 g) dried bread cubes *(far left)*

5 tablespoons (3 fl oz/ 80 ml) extra-virgin olive oil

3 cloves garlic, 2 unpeeled and 1 crushed and minced

6 large, ripe tomatoes, coarsely chopped

3 tablespoons red wine vinegar

Salt and freshly ground pepper

FOR THE CHICKEN BITES:

1 cup (4 oz/125 g) dried bread crumbs *(far left)*

3 skinless, boneless chicken breast halves, cut into 1-inch (2.5-cm) cubes

Vegetable oil for deep-frying

½ cup (½ oz/15 g) fresh basil leaves, coarsely chopped

SLENDER GREEN BEANS IN PESTO

FOR THE PESTO:

3 cloves garlic

2 cups (2 oz/60 g) fresh basil leaves, coarsely chopped

¾ cup (3 oz/90 g) grated Parmesan cheese

¼ cup (1½ oz/45 g) pine nuts or blanched almonds, toasted (page 109), plus extra for garnish

½ cup (4 fl oz/125 ml) extra-virgin olive oil

Salt

1¼ lb (625 g) slender green beans such as haricots verts or baby Blue Lakes, trimmed

To make the pesto, in a blender or mini food processor, combine the garlic, basil, cheese, pine nuts, and about 3 tablespoons of the olive oil. Purée to make a paste. With the motor running, pour in the remaining olive oil in a slow, steady stream, adding only enough to form a thick paste. At the last minute, add 1 teaspoon salt. (If desired, the pesto can be made in the traditional way, using a mortar and pestle, in which case you must first crush together the garlic and salt and then add the basil, cheese, and nuts, grinding them together with the pestle. Finally, slowly pour the oil into the mixture as you work with the pestle.) Set the pesto aside.

Place the beans on a steamer rack over boiling water, cover the steamer, and steam until the beans are just tender, 3–4 minutes. Rinse immediately under cold running water to stop the cooking, then drain and pat dry.

Arrange the beans on a serving dish and spoon as much pesto as desired over them. Serve at room temperature, garnished with the remaining nuts. Any leftover pesto may be stored in the refrigerator. Cover the pesto with a film of olive oil, wrap the container tightly, and store for up to 3 days.

Serving Tip: Serve these beans as part of an antipasto spread, along with black olives, olive oil–dressed boiled potatoes, and roasted and peeled red bell peppers (capsicums) (page 113). Accompany with a basket of bread sticks.

MAKES 4 SERVINGS

PESTO FOR VEGETABLES

Genoese pesto is a classic uncooked sauce made with fresh basil, nuts, garlic, olive oil, and Parmesan cheese. Many cooks think of pesto only with pasta, but in Italy (and Provence, where it is known as *pistou*) the sauce is used on vegetables as well. Try it spooned over potatoes, beets, carrots, or cauliflower. Pine nuts are typically used in the sauce as a thickener, but some-times they are replaced by almonds, walnuts, or even bread crumbs, and each choice gives this classic recipe a slightly different and wonderful flavor.

CORN AND TOMATO SALSA ON CRISPY CORN TORTILLAS

(left)

Cut the kernels off each ear of corn *(left)*. In a large bowl, mix the kernels with the tomatoes, onion, cilantro, basil, chile, lime juice, 1 teaspoon salt, and ½ teaspoon pepper. Mix well.

Pour corn oil into a frying pan to a depth of 1½ inches (4 cm) and heat until it registers 375°F (190°C) on a deep-frying thermometer. Slip 1 tortilla into the hot oil and fry, turning once, until crisp, about 1½ minutes on each side. Using tongs, transfer the tortilla to paper towels to drain and cool. Repeat with 5 more tortillas, letting the oil return to 375°F (190°C) before frying each tortilla.

Cut the remaining 3 tortillas into strips a generous ½ inch (12 mm) wide. Add the strips to the hot oil, in batches, and fry, turning once or twice, until crisp, about 3 minutes total. Transfer to paper towels to drain and cool. Sprinkle the strips evenly with salt.

To serve, place the whole fried tortillas on individual plates and heap the corn salsa on them evenly. Top each serving with a few slices of avocado, a dollop of sour cream, a handful of the tortilla strips, and a sprinkling of chile powder if desired. Serve at once.

Variation Tips: This dish can be made into an appetizer by cutting all 9 corn tortillas into quarters, to produce 36 triangles, and frying them as directed for the whole tortillas. Arrange them on a tray, spoon an equal amount of the corn salsa onto each triangle, and top each with a small piece of avocado and a dab of sour cream. Or, for a light main course to serve 3 people, prepare as directed in the main recipe and serve 2 salsa-topped tortillas to each diner.

MAKES 6 SERVINGS

CUTTING CORN OFF THE COB

Holding an ear of corn by its pointed end, stand it upright and slightly angled, resting its stem end in the bottom of a wide bowl. Using a sharp knife, cut down the length of the cob, taking off 3 or 4 rows of kernels at a time and rotating the ear slightly with each cut. Cut as close to the cob as possible. Continue until all the kernels have been removed.

3 ears of white corn, husks and silk removed

5 tomatoes, finely chopped

⅓ cup (2 oz/60 g) minced red onion

⅓ cup (½ oz/15 g) minced fresh cilantro (fresh coriander)

3 tablespoons minced fresh basil

2 tablespoons minced Anaheim or other medium-hot chile

Juice of 3 limes

Salt and freshly ground pepper

Corn oil for deep-frying

9 corn tortillas

1 avocado, pitted, peeled, and sliced

½ cup (4 oz/125 g) sour cream

Chile powder for sprinkling (optional)

THAI-STYLE GRILLED BEEF SALAD

2 cloves garlic, minced

2 Thai chiles or 1 serrano chile, minced

⅓ cup (3 fl oz/80 ml) fresh lime juice

1 tablespoon water

1 tablespoon soy sauce

3 tablespoons vegetable oil

1 teaspoon brown sugar

4 cups (6 oz/185 g) torn red- or green-leaf lettuce leaves (bite-sized pieces)

1 cup (2 oz/60 g) bean sprouts

½ cup (2½ oz/75 g) finely shredded carrot, preferably cut on a mandoline

½ cup (½ oz/15 g) fresh basil leaves, left whole if small and torn into pieces if large

½ cup (¾ oz/20 g) minced fresh mint, plus several sprigs

½ cup (½ oz/15 g) fresh cilantro (fresh coriander) leaves

1 lb (500 g) beef sirloin or tri-tip

Salt and freshly ground pepper

Prepare a fire in a grill, or preheat the broiler (grill). In a small bowl, mix together the garlic, chiles, lime juice, water, soy sauce, 2 tablespoons of the vegetable oil, and the brown sugar. Set aside.

In a large bowl, combine the lettuce, bean sprouts, carrot, basil, minced mint, and cilantro and toss together. Spread the mixture on a platter.

Rub the meat on both sides with the remaining 1 tablespoon vegetable oil. Place on the grill rack or on a broiler pan and cook, turning once, until seared on both sides, about 1 minute on each side. Transfer to a cutting board and season to taste with salt and pepper. Cut against the grain into strips ¼ inch (6 mm) thick.

Arrange the beef strips over the lettuce mixture and pour the garlic mixture evenly over the top. Garnish with the mint sprigs if desired and serve hot.

Variation Tip: This salad can also be eaten wrapped in a lettuce leaf. Use 2 cups (3 oz/90 g) torn leaves, and keep 8–12 leaves whole. Toss the torn leaves and other ingredients with only half of the sauce, and put the rest of the sauce in a small bowl for dipping. To eat, place a leaf in the palm of your hand and fill it with some of the salad and meat, then fold the bottom of the leaf around the salad. Fold the sides over and then roll up loosely and eat out of hand, after first dipping it in the remaining sauce.

MAKES 4–6 SERVINGS

THAI CHILES

Also called bird chiles, these tiny, slender hot peppers are used both fresh and dried in Thai cooking. In the market, they can be found green, or still immature, and red, fully mature. The heat of Thai chiles is quite intense. When preparing these or any chiles, be careful not to touch your eyes or mouth; consider wearing rubber gloves to protect your hands. The thin membranes inside the chiles are carriers of capsaicin, which is what makes chiles hot. The membranes transfer this heat to the seeds, so removing them both will reduce the fire.

NECTARINE, MELON, AND BLACKBERRY
SALAD WITH FRESH MINT

Halve, pit, and thinly slice the nectarines. Halve and seed the cantaloupe, and place each half, cut side down, on a work surface. Carefully cut away the peel, then cut the melon flesh into 1-inch (2.5-cm) cubes.

In a bowl, combine the nectarine slices and melon cubes. Add the lemon juice and gently mix the fruits with a large spoon. Add all but 4 or 5 of the berries and all but about 1 teaspoon of the mint, and again mix gently. Garnish with the reserved berries and mint and serve immediately.

Serving Tip: For individual servings, put the mixed nectarine and cantaloupe in tulip glasses or small bowls after adding the lemon juice and most of the mint. Top these individual servings with the berries and the remaining mint, and let each person toss his or her own salad.

MAKES 4 SERVINGS

3 white or yellow nectarines

1 small cantaloupe

1 tablespoon fresh lemon juice

1 cup (4 oz/125 g) blackberries

2 tablespoons julienned fresh mint leaves

HANDLING BERRIES

Fresh berries are delicate and should be handled with care. Do not wash berries until just before you plan to use them, as prolonged exposure to moisture will encourage mold. Gently rinse berries, but do not soak them for any length of time. If they absorb too much water, they will become mushy. Keep berries refrigerated until using. If you don't plan to use the berries within 1–2 days, rinse and dry them completely and then freeze them for up to 8 months.

AUTUMN

With the arrival of the cooler days of autumn, salads change mood, moving toward warm combinations of sturdier and more robust fruits and vegetables. Heartier dressings, enhanced with such rich ingredients as aged cheeses, full-flavored vinegars, and honey, signal the season's move away from summer's light hand.

PERSIMMON, HONEY-GLAZED CHICKEN, AND PEPPERY GREENS

Preheat the oven to 350°F (180°C). In a small bowl, stir together the 2 tablespoons honey, oyster sauce, and lemon juice and set aside to allow the flavors to blend.

In another small bowl, stir together the remaining 1 teaspoon honey, the vinegar, peanut oil, and sesame oil. Set aside.

Rub the chicken breasts with salt and pepper to taste and place, skin side up, on a baking sheet. Roast for about 30 minutes. Remove from the oven and remove and discard the skin. Keeping the chicken meat side up, baste the breasts with the honey–oyster sauce mixture and continue to cook, basting several more times with the pan drippings, until the chicken is opaque throughout, about 15 minutes longer. Remove from the oven, turn the chicken pieces meat side down in the pan juices, and set aside.

Put the cabbage, bok choy, watercress, carrot, and chopped cilantro in a bowl. Pour the honey-vinegar mixture over all and turn to coat evenly. Add all but 4 or 5 of the persimmon slices and turn again.

Cut the chicken meat from the bones and into bite-sized cubes. Add them to the bowl, mixing to distribute evenly. Spoon into a serving bowl. Garnish with the reserved persimmon slices and the cilantro sprigs. Serve at once.

Variation Tip: Instead of the slightly pungent napa cabbage, use regular green head cabbage or a mixture of the two.

MAKES 6 SERVINGS

PERSIMMON VARIETIES

The Fuyu persimmon is shaped like a flattened globe and remains firm even when the skin is dark orange and the persimmon is ready to eat. The Hachiya persimmon is the larger, more familiar heart-shaped fruit. Its flesh does not become sweet until the persimmon is quite soft, almost pulpy to the touch. The latter is good for desserts and baking, but it is the crisp Fuyu that is commonly used in salads.

2 tablespoons plus
1 teaspoon honey

1 teaspoon oyster sauce

1 teaspoon fresh
lemon juice

½ cup (4 fl oz/125 ml)
rice vinegar

2 teaspoons peanut oil

¼ teaspoon Asian
sesame oil

3 bone-in chicken breast
halves

Salt and pepper

½ head napa cabbage,
shredded

2 baby bok choy, trimmed
and sliced lengthwise

1 cup (1 oz/30 g) packed
watercress leaves or red
Asian mustard greens
(tough stems removed)

⅓ cup (1½ oz/45 g)
shredded carrot

¼ cup (⅓ oz/10 g)
chopped fresh cilantro
(fresh coriander), plus
several sprigs

3 Fuyu persimmons,
seeded if necessary
and thinly sliced

MUSHROOMS AND FENNEL
WITH PARMESAN CRISPS

2-oz (60-g) block Parmesan cheese

1½ small to medium fennel bulbs

½ lb (250 g) firm fresh white button or cremini mushrooms, brushed clean (see Note)

3 tablespoons fresh lemon juice

3 tablespoons extra-virgin olive oil

Salt and freshly ground pepper

4 tablespoons (⅓ oz/10 g) chopped fresh flat-leaf (Italian) parsley

4 cups (4 oz/125 g) mixed young, tender lettuce leaves

Preheat the broiler (grill). Line a baking sheet with parchment (baking) paper. Using a sharp knife or a mandoline, slice the cheese very thinly *(right)*. Arrange the cheese slices in a single layer on the prepared baking sheet. Place under the broiler about 6 inches (15 cm) from the heat source. Broil (grill) until the cheese slices become crisp and lightly golden, like potato chips, 6–8 minutes. They should no longer be pliable and should lift easily from the baking sheet. Set aside.

Trim away the stalks and the stem ends of the fennel, as well as any brown spots. Using a sharp knife or a mandoline, cut the fennel lengthwise into very thin slices. Set aside. Again using a sharp knife or a mandoline, cut the mushrooms lengthwise into very thin slices.

Put the fennel and mushrooms in a bowl. Add the lemon juice, olive oil, ½ teaspoon salt, 1 teaspoon pepper, and 3 tablespoons of the parsley. Mix to coat well.

Line a serving platter with the lettuce. Spoon the fennel mixture on top of the lettuce leaves, sprinkle with the remaining 1 tablespoon parsley, and surround with the Parmesan crisps. Serve immediately.

Note: The mushrooms for this recipe must be very fresh and tightly closed, with no gills exposed.

Variation Tip: Very thinly sliced celery can be substituted for the fennel in this recipe. Like fennel, celery is crisp and clean tasting. Several anchovy fillets could be added as well.

MAKES 4 SERVINGS

THIN SLICING

With practice, paper-thin slicing can be done with a very sharp knife. Hold the vegetable with fingertips bent slightly under to keep them safely away from the blade. To make very thin slices with ease, however, use a stainless-steel French mandoline, a sturdy tool with an adjustable blade. Many models have two blades, one serrated and one straight, and include a hand guard for extra protection. Asian slicers or shredders of similar design are available, usually made of plastic.

APPLES AND WALNUTS WITH STILTON CHEESE

Put one-third of the cheese in the bottom of a large bowl. Add the olive oil and, using a fork, mash together the cheese and oil. Add the vinegar and continue to mash and to mix. Add the cream and 1 teaspoon pepper and mix well to make a thick, chunky dressing.

Add the apples, sliced celery, currants, and lemon juice to the dressing and mix well. Crumble the remaining cheese and sprinkle it over the salad along with half of the walnuts. Mix them into the salad gently and evenly.

Transfer the salad to a serving bowl and garnish with the remaining walnuts and the celery leaves. Serve at once.

MAKES 6 SERVINGS

PAIRING WALNUTS

This salad takes advantage of two classic pairings: walnuts with Stilton cheese and walnuts with apples. Another fruit that goes well with walnuts are pears, so if the market has stocked beautiful pears—Bosc, red Bartlett (Williams'), Anjou— you can use them in place of the apples. Other blue-veined cheeses such as Maytag, bleu d'Auvergne, or Danish blue can be substituted for the Stilton.

6 oz (185 g) Stilton cheese

1 tablespoon extra-virgin olive oil

1 tablespoon red wine vinegar

2 tablespoons heavy (double) cream

Freshly ground pepper

6 sweet eating apples such as Braeburn, Gala, or Red Delicious, unpeeled, cored and cut into ½-inch (12-mm) dice

4 celery stalks, thinly sliced, plus several whole celery leaves for garnish

2 tablespoons dried currants or raisins

1 tablespoon fresh lemon juice

½ cup (2 oz/60 g) coarsely chopped walnuts, toasted (page 109)

WARM POTATO SALAD
WITH BALSAMIC VINEGAR

6 slices bacon

2 lb (1 kg) small waxy
potatoes such as Yukon
gold, Yellow Finn, or Red
Rose

Salt and freshly ground
pepper

1 small red onion, minced

⅓ cup (2 oz/60 g) finely
chopped celery

2 tablespoons chopped
fresh flat-leaf (Italian)
parsley

2 tablespoons minced
fresh chives, plus several
longer chive lengths

¼ cup (2 fl oz/60 ml)
balsamic vinegar

½ cup (4 fl oz/125 ml)
chicken broth

2 tablespoons red
wine vinegar

1 teaspoon sugar

In a frying pan over medium heat, fry the bacon until crisp, about 6 minutes. Transfer the bacon slices to paper towels to drain. When cool, crumble and set aside. Pour off all but 2 tablespoons of the bacon drippings from the pan and set the pan aside.

In a large saucepan, combine the potatoes, 2 teaspoons salt, and water to cover by 2 inches (5 cm). Bring to a boil over medium-high heat, reduce the heat to medium, and cook, uncovered, until the potatoes are tender and can be easily pierced with a fork, 20–25 minutes. Drain and, when just cool enough to handle, cut into slices about ¼ inch (6 mm) thick.

Place the warm potato slices on a platter in 2 or 3 layers. Sprinkle the crumbled bacon, the onion, the celery, the parsley, and the minced chives over them.

Reheat the bacon fat in the frying pan over medium heat just enough to warm it through. Add the balsamic vinegar and deglaze the pan, scraping up any bits clinging to the bottom. Add the chicken broth, red wine vinegar, sugar, ½ teaspoon salt, and 1 teaspoon pepper and bring to a boil. Pour about half of the hot balsamic mixture over the potatoes, turning them gently so they don't break or mash. Add the rest of the balsamic mixture, garnish with the chive lengths, and serve immediately.

Note: There are many versions of warm potato salad, sometimes called German potato salad. Some of them omit the bacon fat, adding instead a little more chicken broth, in which case the salad can also be served cold. For a traditional cold potato salad with mayonnaise, see page 14.

MAKES 6 SERVINGS

BALSAMIC VINEGAR

A specialty of Modena, Italy, true balsamic vinegar is made from white Trebbiano grapes and is long aged in a series of wooden casks. Labeled *aceto balsamico tradizionale,* it must be aged for at least twelve years and sometimes far longer. Because of its intense flavor and syrupy consistency, it is used very sparingly as a condiment in a finished dish. Although much of the balsamic vinegar available is not true *tradizionale* balsamic, a lesser balsamic vinegar can still be of high quality and make a superb salad dressing.

ROASTED RED PEPPERS
WITH WILD RICE AND ANCHOVIES

In a saucepan over medium-high heat, combine the water and 1 teaspoon salt and bring to a boil. Add the wild rice, let the water return to a boil, then reduce the heat to low, cover, and cook until the rice has absorbed the water and many of the kernels have split, 20–25 minutes. Remove from the heat and let stand, covered, to steam for about 15 minutes.

Transfer the rice to a bowl. Add the sherry and red wine vinegars, green onion, anchovies, all but 1 tablespoon of the bell peppers, ½ teaspoon pepper, and the chopped parsley. Add 3 tablespoons of the olive oil and gently mix. If it seems a little dry, add the remaining 1 tablespoon olive oil. Cover and let stand for 1 hour before serving, to let the flavors blend.

Transfer the salad to a serving bowl or platter. Place the remaining bell pepper in the center and garnish with the parsley sprigs. Serve at room temperature or slightly chilled.

Serving Tip: Because of its pronounced anchovy flavor, this salad is best served in smaller portions as a first course, perhaps accompanied with a crusty baguette and a bowl of olives.

MAKES 4 SERVINGS

WILD RICE

Wild rice is not a true rice, but rather the grain of a marsh grass. Native Americans have long gathered it from lakes in the northern United States, where it grows wild. Today, large commercial crops are cultivated as well, principally by farmers in the great basin of California's Sacramento River, in the Midwest, and in Canada. Wild rice is cooked similarly to ordinary rice, usually steamed or boiled, and then sometimes combined with white or brown rice.

3 cups (24 fl oz/750 ml) water

Salt and freshly ground pepper

1 cup (6 oz/185 g) wild rice

1 tablespoon sherry vinegar

1 teaspoon red wine vinegar

¼ cup (¾ oz/20 g) chopped green (spring) onion, including tender green parts

6 anchovy fillets, preferably olive oil packed, minced

2 red bell peppers (capsicums), roasted and peeled (page 113), then chopped

¼ cup (⅓ oz/10 g) chopped fresh flat-leaf (Italian) parsley, plus 1 or 2 sprigs

3–4 tablespoons (1½–2 fl oz/45–60 ml) olive oil

SWISS CHARD WITH PANCETTA AND HARD-BOILED EGGS

2 bunches Swiss chard

Salt and freshly ground black pepper

¼ lb (125 g) pancetta or thick-sliced bacon, coarsely chopped

3 tablespoons extra-virgin olive oil

1 clove garlic, minced

4 tablespoons (2 fl oz / 60 ml) balsamic vinegar

2 tablespoons red wine vinegar

4 tablespoons (⅓ oz /10 g) chopped fresh flat-leaf (Italian) parsley

5 peeled hard-boiled eggs (page 13), 3 coarsely chopped and 2 cut length-wise into 6 wedges

½ teaspoon cayenne pepper

Cut out the ribs from the chard leaves, cutting well into each leaf to remove all the rib. Trim the rib ends, then chop the ribs into small pieces. Bring a large saucepan three-fourths full of water to a boil over medium-high heat. Add 1 teaspoon salt and the chopped ribs and cook until just tender, 7 minutes. Using a slotted spoon, lift out the ribs, draining them well, and set aside. Add the leaves to the same boiling water and cook just until tender to the bite, 5 minutes. Drain and rinse under cold running water until cool. Gently squeeze the leaves dry with your hands, then coarsely chop them. Gently squeeze them in your hands again. Set aside.

Place a frying pan over medium heat. When it is hot, add the pancetta and cook, turning occasionally, until nearly golden, 5 minutes. (If using bacon, pour off the rendered fat at this point.) Add 1 tablespoon of the olive oil and the garlic and continue to cook until the pancetta and garlic are golden. Using a slotted spoon, transfer the pancetta and garlic to a paper towel to drain.

Add 2 tablespoons of the balsamic vinegar to the frying pan over medium heat and deglaze it, stirring to scrape up bits from the pan bottom. Pour into the bottom of a bowl. Add 1 tablespoon of the remaining balsamic vinegar, 1 tablespoon of the red wine vinegar, and the remaining 2 tablespoons olive oil to the bowl and mix well. Add the chard leaves and ribs, the pancetta and garlic, 3 tablespoons of the parsley, the remaining 1 tablespoon each balsamic vinegar and red wine vinegar, and ½ teaspoon black pepper. Mix well. Add the chopped eggs and gently mix them in.

Transfer to a serving bowl and garnish with the remaining 1 table-spoon parsley, egg wedges, and cayenne. Serve immediately.

MAKES 4 OR 5 SERVINGS

SWISS CHARD

In Italy and France, chard with big, wide ribs—ribs wider than the green of the leaf—are favored. This is because the rib, or stem, is considered a vegetable on its own, often cooked and then dressed with olive oil and garlic and served as a side dish. Other varieties of chard have thinner ribs (in a range of colors) and more leaf. The wider and thicker the rib, the longer it will need to cook to become tender. Even if the ribs are thin, separating them from the leaf and chopping them will give your dish a better texture and flavor.

BRUSSELS SPROUTS
WITH WALNUTS AND ARUGULA

In a saucepan, combine the Brussels sprouts, apple juice, water, and 1 teaspoon salt. Bring to a boil over medium-high heat, reduce the heat to low, cover, and cook just until the sprouts are tender yet firm when pierced at the base, about 15 minutes. Drain well.

As soon as the Brussels sprouts can be handled, cut them lengthwise into thin slices. Put the slices in a bowl and add the walnut oil, vinegar, ¼ teaspoon salt, and ½ teaspoon pepper and gently mix them together.

Divide the arugula among individual plates. Spoon the Brussels sprouts and their dressing over the arugula and garnish with the walnuts. Serve while still warm.

Serving Tip: Instead of serving this salad on individual plates as a first course, try spooning it alongside roasted turkey, chicken, or pork as a warm side dish.

MAKES 4 SERVINGS

1 lb (500 g) Brussels sprouts, trimmed

2 cups (16 fl oz/500 ml) apple juice

1 cup (8 fl oz/250 ml) water

Salt and freshly ground pepper

1½ tablespoons walnut oil

1 tablespoon cider vinegar

1 cup (1 oz/30 g) young, tender arugula (rocket) leaves

½ cup (2 oz/60 g) chopped walnuts, toasted (page 109)

WALNUT OIL

Walnut oils vary greatly in quality and in composition. The best oils are pressed from crushed and lightly toasted nuts. Lesser oils are made of walnut oil mixed with a mild, flavorless oil. Walnut oil has a rather short shelf life, only 6–8 months. After that time, even when stored properly in a cool, dark place, it begins to turn rancid. To forestall spoilage, always check the date of the pressing on the label when shopping for walnut oil to make sure it's fairly fresh, and store the oil in the refrigerator.

WINTER

Winter is the season of visitors and holiday celebrations, and a return to home-cooked meals. Hearty salads are welcome table fare for casual gatherings of friends and family. But salads can also make their appearance at special holiday meals, featuring elegant ingredients like duck breast, salmon fillet, and citrus fruit.

MIXED CITRUS
WITH RED ONIONS AND ESCAROLE
74

POACHED RED TROUT ON WATERCRESS
WITH BLOOD ORANGE DRESSING
77

DUCK BREAST WITH RADICCHIO
AND BITTER GREENS
78

ROASTED BEETS AND PECANS
WITH CURLY ENDIVE
81

ROASTED SALMON WITH CRUMBLED
BACON AND ARUGULA
82

TURKEY AND CELERY SALAD
WITH DRIED CHERRIES
85

ORANGES AND CARROTS
WITH PISTACHIOS
86

MIXED CITRUS
WITH RED ONIONS AND ESCAROLE

BITTER CHICORIES

Escarole (Batavian endive), a
leafy green, belongs to the
same chicory family as frilly-
leaved curly endive (chicory),
purple radicchio, and pale
Belgian endive (chicory/witloof).
Like all these chicories, escarole
is slightly bitter, which is why it
pairs so well with the rich
flavors of toasted nuts, cheese,
and salted meats, as well as
the sweetly acidic taste of
citrus fruits. For eating raw,
the pale yellow inner heart is
best. These leaves are tender
and less bitter than the dark
green outer leaves, which
are usually cooked.

Cut the onion half into paper-thin slices, then cut each slice in half. Set aside.

Cut a slice off the top and bottom of the grapefruit, then stand it upright. Following the contour of the fruit, slice off the peel and white pith in thick strips. Holding the fruit over a bowl, cut along each side of the membranes between the sections, letting each freed section and any juices drop into the bowl. Cut each section in half crosswise. Repeat with the orange and mandarins, then set the citrus aside.

Put the cheese in the bottom of a large bowl and add the olive oil. Using a fork, mash the cheese into the oil until well blended. Stir in the vinegar, ½ teaspoon salt, and ½ teaspoon pepper. Add the escarole leaves and gently mix to coat evenly. Add all the citrus and their juices, the red onion, and the minced chervil and gently mix to coat evenly.

Sprinkle with the chervil sprigs and serve at once.

Variation Tip: Instead of blue cheese, add cubes of Gruyère and 1 ounce (30 g) of prosciutto that has been cut into fine slivers.

MAKES 6 SERVINGS

½ red onion

1 grapefruit

1 orange

2 mandarin oranges

1 oz (30 g) Maytag or other blue cheese

¼ cup (2 fl oz/60 ml) extra-virgin olive oil

2 tablespoons red wine vinegar

Salt and freshly ground pepper

4 cups (12 oz/375 g) torn escarole (Batavian endive) leaves (bite-sized pieces)

¼ cup (⅓ oz/10 g) minced fresh chervil, plus several whole sprigs

POACHED RED TROUT ON WATERCRESS WITH BLOOD ORANGE DRESSING

1 cup (8 fl oz/250 ml) dry white wine

1 cup (8 fl oz/250 ml) water

4 lemon slices, plus 1 teaspoon fresh lemon juice

1 teaspoon fresh minced tarragon leaves

Salt

¾ lb (375 g) skinless red trout or other trout fillets

Juice of 3 blood oranges (about ¾ cup/6 fl oz/ 180 ml), plus 1 whole blood orange

2 teaspoons extra-virgin olive oil

1 teaspoon minced shallot

4 cups (4 oz/125 g) watercress sprigs (about 2 bunches), tough stems removed

In a frying pan, combine the wine, water, lemon slices, tarragon, and ½ teaspoon salt. Place over medium-high heat and bring to just below a boil. The water should be barely rippling. Add the trout fillets and poach, keeping the liquid at just below a simmer, until the fillets are just opaque throughout, 3–4 minutes. Using a slotted spoon, transfer the fillets to a plate and set aside.

In a saucepan over medium heat, combine the orange and lemon juices and bring to a boil. Boil until reduced to about ½ cup (4 fl oz/125 ml). Remove from the heat and let cool. Stir in the olive oil and the shallot.

Cut a slice off the top and bottom of the blood orange, then stand it upright. Following the contour of the fruit, slice off the peel and white pith in thick strips. Slice the orange crosswise and remove any seeds. Set aside.

Put the watercress sprigs in a bowl and pour all but 2 tablespoons of the orange-juice mixture over them. Gently mix to coat evenly. Divide the watercress evenly among individual bowls or plates.

Break each trout fillet into several pieces and arrange the pieces on top of the dressed greens. Drizzle each with a little of the reserved orange-juice mixture. Garnish each salad with a slice or two of blood orange and serve at once.

Serving Tip: If blood oranges are not available, substitute navel oranges and use raspberry vinegar instead of lemon juice.

MAKES 4 SERVINGS

USING BLOOD ORANGES

Blood oranges can be used just like other oranges, even though their flavor is sweeter than that of navels or Valencias, the two types most commonly stocked in markets. Use them for juice, for sorbets, in salads, and for sauces, where their unusual color can be shown off. When making a salad, remember that the juice stains all that it touches a brilliant red. If you want to keep colors separate, add the blood oranges at the last minute, just before serving.

DUCK BREAST WITH RADICCHIO AND BITTER GREENS

In a bowl, whisk together the lemon juice, vinegar, ½ teaspoon salt, and ¼ teaspoon pepper. Slowly drizzle in the olive oil while whisking, to make a thick vinaigrette.

Using a sharp knife, cut away the hard white core from the base of the radicchio. Cut the head lengthwise into slices ¼ inch (6 mm) thick, then separate the layers and remove the hard V-shaped core. Put the cut radicchio into the bowl holding the vinaigrette. Add the arugula, watercress, and parsley and gently mix. Set aside.

Pat the duck breast dry. In a frying pan over high heat, warm ½ teaspoon salt. When it is hot, add the duck breast, skin side down. Reduce the heat to medium-high and cook until crisp and golden brown on the first side, 6–7 minutes. Turn over and cook the other side until lightly browned, about 4 minutes. Cover the pan and cook until the duck breast is medium-rare, another 3–4 minutes. Drain briefly on paper towels.

Transfer the duck breast to a cutting board and use a knife to separate the breast halves. Cut each breast half crosswise into slices ¼ inch (6 mm) thick.

Heap the dressed radicchio mixture in a bowl or on a platter, fluffing up the middle, and arrange the duck slices on top of it, giving them a final sprinkling of pepper. Serve while the duck is still warm.

Serving Tip: A full-bodied red wine such as a Barbera from Italy or a Syrah from France wonderfully complements the rich flavor of the duck and the bitter flavor of the greens.

MAKES 4 SERVINGS

COOKING DUCK BREAST

Duck breast has a fairly thick, fatty skin. When the breast is seared, some of the fat melts away, flavoring the meat in the process, and the skin turns a lovely golden brown. To accomplish this, cook the breast skin side down to start, as this speeds the fat-melting process without overcooking the breast. (The meat should be at least pink, if not deep rose, when done.) Once the skin is brown, turn the breast over to allow the meat to cook in the rendered fat. If desired, remove the skin before serving.

3 tablespoons fresh lemon juice

1 teaspoon Champagne vinegar

Salt and freshly ground pepper

2 tablespoons olive oil

2 small heads radicchio

1 cup (1 oz/30 g) baby arugula (rocket) leaves

½ cup (½ oz/15 g) water-cress, red Asian mustard greens, or dandelion leaves (bite-sized pieces) or additional whole baby arugula (rocket) leaves

2 tablespoons chopped fresh flat-leaf (Italian) parsley

1 whole boneless duck breast

ROASTED BEETS AND PECANS
WITH CURLY ENDIVE

6 small beets

2 tablespoons extra-virgin olive oil, plus extra for rubbing on beets

¼ cup (2 fl oz/60 ml) balsamic vinegar

Salt and freshly ground pepper

4 cups (12 oz/375 g) torn curly endive (chicory) leaves, pale inner leaves only (bite-sized pieces)

1 cup (1 oz/30 g) watercress sprigs (about ½ bunch)

¼ cup (¼ oz/7 g) grated orange zest

¾ cup (3 oz/90 g) coarsely chopped pecans, toasted (page 109)

Preheat the oven to 350°F (180°C). If the greens are still attached to the beets, cut them off, leaving about 1 inch (2.5 cm) of the stem intact, and reserve the greens for another use. Lightly oil the unpeeled beets with olive oil and place in a baking pan. Roast, turning occasionally, until tender when pierced with a fork, 40–45 minutes. Remove and let stand until cool enough to handle, then peel and cut into rounds ¼ inch (6 mm) thick. Place in a bowl, cover to keep warm, and set aside.

In a small bowl, whisk together the vinegar, ¼ teaspoon salt, and ½ teaspoon pepper. Slowly drizzle in the 2 tablespoons olive oil while whisking, to make a thick vinaigrette.

Divide the curly endive and watercress among individual plates. Top with the beet rounds and drizzle with the vinaigrette. Garnish with the orange zest and the toasted pecans. Serve at once.

Variation Tip: For an extra garnish, add a spoonful or two of crumbled fresh goat cheese.

MAKES 4 SERVINGS

COOKING WITH BEETS

Beets are now available in a range of colors, including gold, though deep red beets remain the most familiar type. The intense color of red beets is due to the presence of a pigment called betanin, which stains anything the beet touches red. This is why beets are said to "bleed." To minimize the bleeding, do not cut into beets before cooking. Instead, leave a bit of the beet greens intact, as well as the root, waiting until after the beets are cooked to trim them. A mixture of golden and red beets is especially attractive in this salad.

ROASTED SALMON WITH CRUMBLED BACON AND ARUGULA

Preheat the oven to 500°F (260°C). In a frying pan over medium heat, fry the bacon until crisp, about 6 minutes. Transfer to paper towels to drain. Let cool, then crumble and set aside.

Pour off all but about 1 tablespoon of the bacon drippings and return the pan to medium-low heat. Add the shallot and sauté for 1–2 minutes, then raise the heat to medium-high. Add the vinegar and deglaze the pan, stirring to scrape up any browned bits from the pan bottom. Add the chicken broth, reduce the heat to low, and simmer for a minute or two. Whisk in the olive oil. Remove from the heat and cover to keep warm.

Cut the salmon fillets in half and rub the pieces on both sides with salt and pepper to taste. Lightly oil a baking dish large enough to accommodate the salmon fillets in a single layer and place them in the prepared dish. Roast in the oven until just opaque when pierced at the center, 13–15 minutes.

While the fish is cooking, divide the arugula and lettuce among individual salad plates, and drizzle with all but 2 tablespoons of the balsamic mixture. When the fish is ready, place a portion on each plate, drizzle with the remaining balsamic mixture, and top evenly with the crumbled bacon. Serve at once.

Variation Tip: For an Italian accent, instead of bacon, use snippets of crisp prosciutto, accomplished by barely sautéing thin strips in a little olive oil.

MAKES 4 SERVINGS

CHOOSING SALMON

Salmon flesh varies in color from red to pale pink, but the texture of the flesh is more important than the color. It should be firm to the touch, not soft, and the skin, if still intact, should be slippery. When purchasing a whole salmon, look for bright eyes. Salmon have a large backbone and plenty of small, needlelike bones in the fish's meaty sides, sometimes still present in fillets. These can be removed before or after cooking with sturdy tweezers or needle-nosed pliers that are kept reserved for kitchen use.

4 slices bacon

2 tablespoons minced shallot

⅓ cup (3 fl oz/80 ml) balsamic vinegar

2 tablespoons chicken broth

1 tablespoon extra-virgin olive oil

2 salmon fillets, each about ½ lb (250 g) and ½–¾ inch (12 mm–2 cm) thick

Salt and freshly ground pepper

2 cups (2 oz/60 g) young, tender arugula (rocket) leaves

2 cups (3 oz/90 g) torn red-leaf lettuce leaves (bite-sized pieces)

TURKEY AND CELERY SALAD WITH DRIED CHERRIES

1 small celery root (celeriac), about ¾ lb (375 g)

4 celery stalks, minced

2 cups (12 oz/375 g) diced cooked turkey or chicken, chilled (see Note)

¼ cup (1½ oz/45 g) pine nuts

¼ cup (1 oz/30 g) dried pitted cherries, halved, or other dried fruits *(far right)*

2 tablespoons light sour cream

2 tablespoons mayonnaise, preferably homemade (page 111)

1 teaspoon Dijon mustard

1½ tablespoons Champagne vinegar

Salt and freshly ground pepper

8–10 lettuce leaves

Using a paring knife, peel the thick skin from the celery root (see page 18). Then, using the large holes on a handheld grater-shredder, shred it into a bowl.

Add the celery, turkey, pine nuts, dried cherries, sour cream, mayonnaise, mustard, vinegar, ½ teaspoon salt, and ½ teaspoon pepper to the celery root and mix well. Cover and refrigerate for at least 1 hour and up to 24 hours before serving.

Line a platter with the lettuce leaves. Mound the turkey mixture atop the lettuce. Serve at once.

Note: For the cooked poultry in this recipe, use leftover roasted turkey or chicken. If you have none on hand, poach some chicken breasts. Put 2 or 3 bone-in chicken breast halves in a large saucepan and add lightly salted water to cover. Bring to a boil over high heat. Reduce the heat to low and simmer for 30 minutes. Remove from the heat and let stand for 30 minutes. Discard the skin and bones and cut the meat into bite-sized pieces.

Serving Tip: This salad, like other turkey or chicken salads or tuna salad, makes an excellent sandwich filling. It is especially good on rye bread or sourdough. It also makes a nice main course for two.

MAKES 4 SERVINGS

DRIED FRUITS IN SALADS

Dried fruits are an excellent pantry item, especially in winter when fresh fruits are not as varied as they are in other seasons. Dried cherries, cranberries, peaches, plums, apricots, pears, and even dried mangoes and pineapple can add a flavorful boost to green salads, pasta salads, and grain-based salads. Chop or julienne larger fruits and halve smaller ones such as cranberries and cherries before adding them.

85

ORANGES AND CARROTS
WITH PISTACHIOS

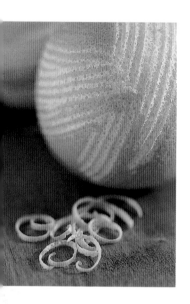

Using the fine shredding blade of a mandoline or the large holes on a handheld grater-shredder, finely shred the carrots.

In a salad bowl, stir together the lemon juice, the sugar, and the Cointreau. Add the carrots and gently mix. Cover and refrigerate this mixture for at least 1 hour or for up to 8 hours to allow the flavors to blend.

Just before serving, using a zester, remove the zest from 1 orange in long, thin ribbons. Cut a slice off the top and bottom of the orange, then stand it upright. Following the contour of the fruit, slice off the peel and white pith in thick strips. Cut the orange crosswise into slices ¼ inch (6 mm) thick. Peel and slice the second orange in the same way.

Add the orange zest and slices to the bowl and mix them gently into the carrots.

Divide the salad among individual bowls or plates. Garnish each serving with an equal amount of the mint and pistachios.

Serving Tip: When serving this salad as a first course, accompany it with something salty, such as a slice of prosciutto or good salami. The saltiness is the perfect foil to the tart sweetness of the oranges.

MAKES 4 SERVINGS

ZESTING CITRUS

Citrus zest, the colored portion of the peel, is rich in aromatic and flavorful oils. When zesting, choose organic fruit if possible and scrub the fruit well to remove any wax or residue. Use only the thin outer layer of the rind, taking care not to include the bitter white pith. Zest may be removed with a zester, a tool designed to remove the zest in thin strips. A vegetable peeler or a paring knife can be used, but will produce pieces that are short, wide, and irregular. Zest may be removed with the fine rasps of a handheld grater as well.

1 lb (500 g) carrots, peeled

Juice of 1 lemon

1 tablespoon sugar

1 teaspoon Cointreau or other orange-flavored liqueur

2 navel oranges

2 tablespoons minced fresh mint

3 tablespoons chopped pistachios

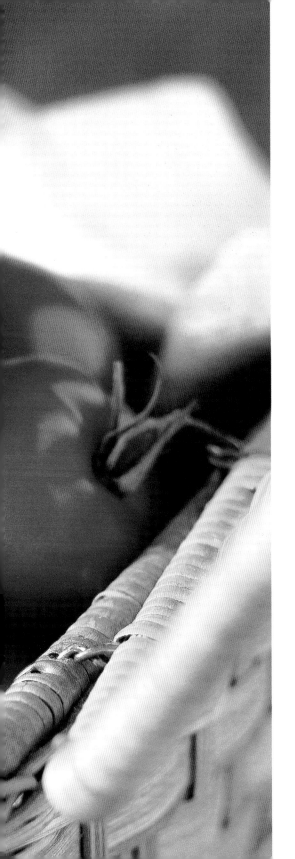

PICNIC SALADS

Half the fun of a picnic or a potluck is to see and to sample what everyone else has brought. Salads are an excellent choice for such affairs because they're relatively easy to make and a lot of variety is possible. Some salads are better suited for transporting than others. The recipes that follow fit the bill: Their flavors improve after sitting, or they can be assembled and dressed easily on-site.

RIGATONI SALAD WITH GREEN CAULIFLOWER, CAPERS, AND SAFFRON

SAFFRON

Saffron is the dried orange-red stigmas of a type of crocus. The autumn-blooming flower is native to eastern Europe and western Asia, although since the Middle Ages it has been cultivated elsewhere in Europe as well and used especially in Spanish cooking. For the best quality, choose saffron threads, or actual stigmas, rather than powdered saffron, which loses its flavor with storage. Saffron is used both for the lovely burnished golden color it gives to a dish and for its slightly bitter yet subtly perfumed flavor.

In a small bowl, stir together 4 tablespoons (2 fl oz/60 ml) of the olive oil, the lemon juice, saffron, cumin, cayenne, and ½ teaspoon salt. Set aside.

Put the cauliflower florets in a steamer basket and sprinkle with ½ teaspoon salt. Place over boiling water, cover, and steam until just tender, 7–8 minutes. The florets should still have a little crunch to them and not be at all mushy. Remove the steamer basket from the pan and place under cold running water to stop the cooking. Drain well.

Bring a large saucepan three-fourths full of water to a boil and add 1 teaspoon salt. Add the rigatoni, stir well, and cook until al dente, 9–10 minutes or according to package directions. Drain and transfer to a large, deep bowl.

Toss the pasta with the remaining 2 tablespoons olive oil. Add the cooled cauliflower and the lemon-juice mixture and turn to coat well. Set aside a few of the parsley leaves for garnish and add the remaining parsley leaves and the thyme to the pasta, turning to distribute evenly. Cover and refrigerate for at least 1 hour or up to 6 hours before serving to allow the flavors to blend.

Bring the salad to room temperature. Garnish with the reserved parsley leaves and the capers and serve.

Variation Tip: Rigatoni is not the only choice for this pasta salad. Try any pasta that has a ridged and irregular shape, such as fusilli, rotelle, or radiatori. These pastas will capture the sauce in their nooks and crannies and infuse the salad with flavor.

MAKES 8 SERVINGS

6 tablespoons (3 fl oz/ 90 ml) extra-virgin olive oil

¼ cup (2 fl oz/60 ml) fresh lemon juice

¼ teaspoon saffron threads

¼ teaspoon ground cumin

⅛ teaspoon cayenne pepper

Salt

1 head green or white cauliflower, stems trimmed and head separated into bite-sized florets

10 oz (315 g) rigatoni

¼ cup (¼ oz/7 g) fresh flat-leaf (Italian) parsley leaves

1 teaspoon minced fresh thyme

2 tablespoons capers, rinsed

TOMATOES WITH ANCHOVIES AND OLIVES

12–14 medium to
large tomatoes, sliced
a generous ¼ inch
(6 mm) thick

24 anchovy fillets,
preferably olive oil packed

¾ cup (4 oz/125 g)
oil-cured black olives

FOR THE VINAIGRETTE:

2 cloves garlic, coarsely
chopped

Salt and freshly ground
pepper

¼ cup (2 fl oz/60 ml)
extra-virgin olive oil

2 tablespoons red wine
vinegar

Fresh flat-leaf (Italian)
parsley sprigs for garnish
(optional)

Arrange the tomatoes in overlapping layers on a platter. Evenly distribute the anchovy fillets over them, then scatter the olives across the top.

To make the vinaigrette, in a bowl or a mortar, combine the garlic and ½ teaspoon salt. Using a fork or a pestle, crush them into a paste. Add the olive oil slowly, beating it in with the fork, and then add the vinegar and ½ teaspoon pepper, mixing well. Put the vinaigrette in a jar and cover tightly.

Shortly before serving, shake the vinaigrette in its jar and pour it over the platter of tomatoes. Garnish with the parsley sprigs if desired.

Serving Tip: If you are taking this salad to a picnic or potluck, consider bringing a cutting board and knife, the tomatoes, the anchovies and olives in containers, and the jar containing the vinaigrette. Then, cut the tomatoes and assemble the salad on-site.

MAKES 8 SERVINGS

ANCHOVY STYLES

Anchovies packed in oil and packed in salt are essentially interchangeable in terms of use, but their textures differ. Salt-packed whole anchovies tend to be firmer than oil-packed fillets. They should be rinsed, skinned if needed by scraping the scales with a knife, and filleted by splitting the fish along the backbone, then lifting out the bones. If the fish is excessively salty, soak it for a few minutes in cool water. Olive oil–packed fillets need only be drained, after rinsing if desired. The oil can supply a positive note to certain dishes, such as this one.

LENTIL SALAD WITH MOZZARELLA AND PROSCIUTTO

There are many different types of lentils, ranging in color from green to brown to red to pink to yellow. In Indian and Middle Eastern cooking, red and yellow are typically used. In India, these lentils are also called *dal,* a term that refers both to the legumes and to the dish made from them. For Mediterranean-style dishes, such as this salad, use the relatively tiny French green lentils (also called *lentilles vertes du Puy* or Puy lentils), as they keep their shape better during cooking than the more familiar brown lentils.

Pick over the lentils, removing any grit or misshapen lentils, then rinse well. In a saucepan over high heat, combine the water and ½ teaspoon salt and bring to a boil. Add the lentils, reduce the heat to medium-low, cover, and cook until the lentils are tender but still hold their shape, 20–25 minutes. Be careful not to over-cook. Remove from the heat and drain well. Let cool to room temperature.

In a bowl, stir together the olive oil, vinegar, ½ teaspoon pepper, onion, 2 tablespoons of the basil, and all but one-fourth of the prosciutto. Add the lentils and mix well.

Spoon the lentils onto a platter. Arrange the mozzarella slices around the edges of the platter, tucking them under the lentils. Sprinkle the remaining minced and whole basil leaves and the prosciutto over the lentils, and serve.

Serving Tip: If you are transporting your dish, slice the mozzarella, then return it to the liquid in which it was packed. This will keep it fresh and moist. Just before serving, add the mozzarella and the garnishes to the platter.

MAKES 6 SERVINGS

1¼ cups (9 oz/280 g) French green lentils

4 cups (32 fl oz/1 l) water

Salt and freshly ground pepper

3 tablespoons extra-virgin olive oil

¼ cup (2 fl oz/60 ml) red wine vinegar

2 tablespoons minced red onion

4 tablespoons (⅓ oz/10 g) julienned fresh basil leaves, plus whole leaves for garnish

¼ lb (125 g) paper-thin prosciutto slices, cut into strips 1 inch (2.5 cm) wide

⅓ lb (155 g) fresh mozzarella cheese, cut into slices a generous ¼ inch (6 mm) thick

ANCHOÏADE WITH RADISHES, FENNEL, CELERY, AND CARROTS

FOR THE ANCHOÏADE:

²/₃ –¾ cup (5–6 fl oz / 160–180 ml) extra-virgin olive oil

4 oz (125 g) anchovy fillets, preferably olive oil packed

5 cloves garlic, crushed and then minced

1 bunch red radishes, trimmed

2 fennel bulbs, trimmed and cut lengthwise into slices ¼ inch (6 mm) thick and ½ inch (12 mm) wide

4 celery stalks, cut into pieces 3 inches (7.5 cm) long and ½ inch (12 mm) thick

4 carrots, peeled and cut into sticks 3 inches (7.5 cm) long and ½ inch (12 mm) thick

To make the *anchoïade,* in a small frying pan over low heat, warm ²/₃ cup olive oil. Add the anchovies and garlic and cook, mashing the anchovies until they dissolve into the oil to make a paste, about 3 minutes. Gradually stir in enough of the remaining oil to give the sauce the consistency of a thick vinaigrette. Alternatively, mash the garlic and anchovies together in a mortar with a pestle or process in a mini food processor to make a paste, then slowly add the olive oil to achieve the proper consistency. Transfer to a small bowl.

Arrange the radishes, fennel, celery, and carrots in a serving bowl or on a platter. Serve accompanied with the *anchoïade.*

Serving Tip: Offer a couple of crusty baguettes or some bread sticks along with the vegetables.

MAKES 8 SERVINGS

ANCHOÏADE

Anchoïade, a thickened sauce of anchovies, olive oil, and garlic, is a traditional Provençal spread for toasts or dipping sauce for raw vegetables. When used as a dip, it is similar to the Italian *bagna cauda,* which is served hot. For dipping in both *anchoïade* and *bagna cauda,* a variety of raw vegetables are used, from common carrots, radishes, fennel, and celery to more unusual black radishes and Jerusalem artichokes. Boiled beets and potatoes are sometimes included as well.

RICE SALAD WITH TUNA AND CAPERS

In a saucepan over high heat, combine the water and ½ teaspoon salt and bring to a boil. Add the rice, bring back to a boil, reduce the heat to low, cover, and cook until the rice is tender and the liquid is absorbed, about 20 minutes. Remove from the heat and let stand, covered, until completely cool, at least 1 hour. Separate the grains with a fork.

Drain the tuna of its excess oil, put it in a bowl, and then flake it with a fork.

In a large bowl, stir together the lemon juice, olive oil, 1 teaspoon salt, and 1 teaspoon pepper. Add the rice, tuna, capers, parsley, chopped basil, and cilantro and mix gently.

Transfer the salad to a serving bowl and garnish with the whole basil leaves.

Serving Tip: To make individual servings, cut large tomatoes in half and scoop them out, leaving a shell. Fill the halves to heaping with the salad and garnish each with a basil sprig.

Make-Ahead Tip: You can cook the rice 1 day in advance of making the salad and refrigerate it. Bring it back to room temperature before assembling and serving the salad.

MAKES 8 SERVINGS

CAPERS

Capers are the small unopened flower buds of a shrub native to the Mediterranean. They are sun-dried and packed in brine or salt, and they bring a pleasant pungent flavor and a light crunch to a variety of dishes. Many consider the smallest variety of capers, called nonpareils, to be the finest. This pickled variety comes from Provence, in southern France. Larger pea-sized capers are also good. Before using, be sure to rinse salted capers in cool water or drain capers packed in brine and gently blot dry with a paper towel.

4 cups (32 fl oz/1 l) water

Salt and freshly ground pepper

2 cups (14 oz/440 g) long-grain white rice

2 cans (6 oz/185 g each) tuna, preferably olive oil packed

¼ cup (2 fl oz/60 ml) fresh lemon juice or white wine vinegar

¼ cup (2 fl oz/60 ml) extra-virgin olive oil

1½ tablespoons capers, rinsed

½ cup (¾ oz/20 g) chopped fresh flat-leaf (Italian) parsley

½ cup (¾ oz/20 g) chopped fresh basil, plus whole leaves for garnish

½ cup (¾ oz/20 g) chopped fresh cilantro (fresh coriander)

COUSCOUS SALAD WITH CHERRY TOMATOES AND BELL PEPPERS

2 cups (16 fl oz/500 ml) water

¼ cup (2 fl oz/60 ml) plus 1 teaspoon extra-virgin olive oil

Salt

2 cups (12 oz/375 g) instant couscous

1½ red bell peppers (capsicums)

1½ cups (9 oz/280 g) mixed red and yellow cherry tomatoes

¼ cup (⅓ oz/10 g) chopped fresh mint, plus whole sprigs for garnish

¼ cup (2 fl oz/60 ml) fresh orange juice

1 tablespoon grated orange zest

3 tablespoons red wine vinegar

In a saucepan over high heat, combine the water, the 1 teaspoon olive oil, and ½ teaspoon salt. Bring to a boil. Pour in the couscous, stirring constantly, and remove from the heat. Cover and let stand for 15 minutes. The liquid will be fully absorbed and the couscous will have plumped.

Meanwhile, roast and peel the bell peppers (see page 113) and chop them coarsely. Stem the cherry tomatoes and halve them lengthwise.

Transfer the couscous to a large serving bowl. Using a fork, fluff the couscous grains to separate them. Add the bell peppers, tomatoes, chopped mint, orange juice, orange zest, ¼ cup olive oil, vinegar, and ½ teaspoon salt. Mix gently but well. Cover and refrigerate for at least 1 hour and up to 12 hours before serving, to allow the flavors to blend.

Garnish with the mint sprigs and serve the salad chilled or at room temperature.

Make-Ahead Tip: Because this salad is best when the flavors have been allowed to blend for several hours, it is a good choice for making in the morning and taking along to a leisurely picnic. It can be carried easily in a covered bowl.

MAKES 8 SERVINGS

COUSCOUS

Although it is commonly mistaken for a grain, couscous is actually tiny pasta made from durum-wheat semolina. In North African countries such as Tunisia and Morocco, where it is a staple, it is traditionally made by hand and then steamed twice in a special two-tiered pot called a *couscousière.* Elsewhere, precooked dried couscous, sometimes called instant couscous, is available either packaged or in bulk. It requires no cooking at all— just rehydrating in boiling water—before serving.

WHITE PEACHES WITH ALMONDS AND CURRANTS

Halve, pit, and slice the peeled peaches. Place them in a large bowl and add the currants.

In a small bowl, stir together the lemon juice and sugar until the sugar dissolves, then pour the mixture over the peaches and the currants. Stir gently to coat evenly, then stir in the almond extract.

Just before serving, sprinkle with the almonds.

Serving Tip: Serve this simple fruit salad as a dessert with a late-harvest Riesling and biscotti.

Make-Ahead Tip: This salad benefits from being made several hours in advance of serving to allow the flavors to blend. It's a good choice for transporting to a picnic or party.

MAKES 8 SERVINGS

10 white peaches, peeled
(far left)

½ cup (3 oz/90 g)
dried currants

3 tablespoons fresh
lemon juice

2 tablespoons sugar

¼ teaspoon almond
extract (essence)

½ cup (2 oz/60 g) sliced
(flaked) or chopped
almonds

PEELING PEACHES

To remove the fuzzy skin of peaches with ease, blanch them first. Bring a large saucepan three-fourths full of water to a boil. Cut a shallow X on the blossom end of each peach. Working in batches, immerse the peaches for 30 seconds. Using a slotted spoon, transfer to a work surface. When cool enough to handle, slip off the skins, using your fingertips or a small, sharp knife.

SALAD BASICS

With their myriad combinations, salads rely on seasonal ingredients perhaps more than any other dish. The great virtue of salads is their inherent versatility and opportunity for creativity; they are ideally made with whichever items in your market or your garden taste the best and look the most appealing.

After trying a few of the recipes in this book, you may be inspired to move beyond their confines to create your own mixtures. The following guidelines will help you create vibrant and memorable combinations.

ELEMENTS OF A SALAD

Reduced to its most elementary form, salad means fresh greens. Sometimes lettuce is the sole ingredient—it may be simply torn or chopped, then tossed with a dressing. Although at first glance many of the greens might appear similar, on closer acquaintance their individual characteristics will become apparent.

MILD LETTUCES

All lettuces are relatively mild in flavor when compared to most other salad greens, but among the various lettuces there are distinct differences in color, taste, shape, and texture. Butter (Boston) lettuce has soft leaves and a sweet, fresh taste. Green leaf is a more crinkly lettuce with good flavor. Pale iceberg is mild and crunchy. The delicate leaves of mâche have a nutty taste. Mild oakleaf lettuce has distinctively notched leaves, while the sturdy, dark green leaves of romaine (cos) are more robustly flavored.

BITTER CHICORIES

Members of the chicory family all share a bitter taste, but their textures, leaf shapes, and degrees of bitterness are very different. Use chicories in combination with mild lettuces to add both flavor and visual appeal. Belgian endive (chicory or witloof) has crisp, cylindrical leaves that are only mildly bitter, while the deep red leaves of radicchio are more pronounced in flavor. Curly endive has frilly, bitter leaves that become milder toward the heart. The ruffled green leaves of escarole (Batavian endive) are slightly bitter.

SPICY GREENS

Spicy greens play an important role in salad making, acting as an accent when mixed with other greens. All contribute a tantalizing piquancy to a salad, but each has a distinct taste and can also be used on its own. The deeply notched leaves of arugula (rocket) are pleasantly peppery, while cress has dark green leaves with a spicy bite. Light-colored mustard greens are pungent and musky, and round nasturtium leaves provide a peppery accent. Peppery watercress leaves are deep green and smooth.

FRESH GREEN HERBS

Herbs are a special category of greens. They can be used both as seasonings and as main ingredients, as they are in Green Herb Salad with Champagne Vinaigrette (page 26). The primary green herbs, discussed below, have little relation to one another in flavor.

Basil has a faint taste of cloves and anise, and chervil a hint of licorice. Cilantro (fresh coriander) is lightly perfumed, nearly sweet, while dill is definitely sweet and a little grassy. Mint is refreshing and sweet, while dainty-leaved thyme has a "clean" flavor. Parsley's taste is also described as "clean," and the flat-leaved variety is more strongly flavored than the curly. Tarragon is

aromatic, almost sharply perfumed, with a sweet anise flavor. Mixing and matching greens or herbs and greens makes for a lively, flavorful but still elegantly simple salad. For example, combine sturdy, slightly bitter escarole with spicy watercress or arugula, or mild butter and red-leaf lettuces with sprigs of chervil or cilantro.

FRUITS AND VEGETABLES

Salads can be made entirely of fruits, as in Ambrosia (page 22), or entirely of vegetables, as in the classic potato or bean salad. However, fruits and vegetables can also be added to mixed green salads, perhaps with cheese and nuts as well. Especially nice combinations include pears with curly endive and blue cheese, and beets with mâche and toasted pecans. The natural sweetness of fruits and vegetables is balanced by the salty flavors of cured meats such as bacon, ham, and sausage, all delicious in combination with fruits as well.

CHEESE

There are hundreds of different cheese varieties, and every one can be used in a salad. Chunks of blue cheese, crumbles of feta, shavings of Parmesan, slivers of Gruyère, dollops of goat cheese, or cubes of Cheddar are just a few of the possibilities.

Parmesan with fennel, Gruyère with bacon and Belgian endive, feta with melons and cilantro, and goat cheese with tomatoes and basil are some examples of excellent cheese pairings.

NUTS AND SEEDS

Nuts and seeds, either raw or toasted, can be an integral part of a salad. Pecans with spicy greens and scallops, sesame seeds with shrimp and lettuce, and almonds with turkey and celery are a few of the best combinations. For instructions on toasting, see page 109.

SALAD DRESSINGS

A good salad dressing should enhance and harmonize with the simple, fresh tastes of a salad. The two main categories of dressings are vinaigrettes and creamy dressings. The first is an emulsion based on oil and an acidic liquid, like vinegar or fruit juice, which do not naturally mix but may be whisked into suspension. Thicker creamy dressings are typically based on mayonnaise (also an emulsion), yogurt, milk, tofu, sour cream, sweet cream, or buttermilk.

The oil you choose, whether a bland one such as sunflower oil or a distinctively flavored one such as olive or walnut oil, will depend on the ingredients in your salad. In other words, you should consider the need for greater or lesser flavor added by the dressing. Infused oils, such as basil or pepper oil, are a good way to add complementary flavor to a salad. Vinegars are typically made from wine or fermented fruits. Red wine, white wine, and balsamic are the most common wine vinegars, but sherry, Champagne, and port wine vinegars are also available, as are cider and malt vinegars.

Minced fresh or crumbled dried herbs, such as basil, oregano, and tarragon, and spices such as cayenne pepper, turmeric, ginger, or anise, can be added to any dressing. Dry or prepared mustard is a common addition, and sugar may be added as well. Vegetable or fruit juices such as tomato, raspberry, or orange add a dramatic flavor dimension, as do minced garlic, shallots, or onions. Simply put, salad dressings can be as creative and varied as salads themselves.

Whatever goes into your salad, in most cases it should be dressed and tossed just moments before serving. Prolonged contact with the dressing will cause leaves to wilt. Notable exceptions are recipes in which the dressing is deliberately used to change the texture or flavor of the ingredients through marination.

PUTTING IT ALL TOGETHER

A salad might well be as simple as torn greens tossed with a basic vinaigrette. A little careful attention to detail can make all the difference between a limp salad with a watery dressing and one that is crisp and flavorful.

CHOOSING GREENS

To select salad greens, look for leaves that are fresh, bright, crisp, and free of blemishes. Avoid any that are wilted or browned. Choose heads that are densely packed and heavy for their size. Grocery stores stock lettuce greens year-round, but during the cool months of spring and autumn, farmers' markets abound with locally grown greens.

WASHING GREENS

To wash salad greens, immerse them in a large bowl or sink filled with cool water. Discard any wilted or yellowed leaves. Lift out the greens gently, and replace the water, repeating until the water is clear. A salad spinner is ideal for drying greens, but shaking them gently in a clean kitchen towel will also absorb excess moisture. Be sure to dry the greens as much as possible, for excess water will dilute the flavor of the dressing.

CRISPING GREENS

If you have the time, put washed greens in the refrigerator to chill and crisp for up to a day. After washing the greens, spread a clean kitchen towel flat. Arrange the leaves in a single layer on the towel and gently roll up the leaves in the towel, jelly-roll fashion. Be careful not to crush the leaves. Loosely cover the roll with a large plastic bag or plastic wrap. When ready to use, unwrap and unroll the lettuce.

PREPARING GREENS

To prepare lettuce and other greens for salad, tear large leaves into bite-sized pieces. Make sure they are small enough to be managed easily with just a fork. Smaller leaves such as baby spinach can be left whole. If a recipe calls for shredded greens, neatly stack several leaves on a cutting surface and, with a sharp knife, cut across the leaves to make strips.

CHOOSING HERBS

When shopping, choose herbs that look bright and healthy and smell fragrant, avoiding those that have wilted, yellowed, or blackened leaves.

STORING HERBS

Delicate fresh herbs require special care during storage. Wrap herbs in damp paper towels, then slip them into a plastic bag and refrigerate for 3–5 days. Be especially gentle with fragile herbs, for they will bruise and discolor easily.

To keep long-stemmed herbs such as parsley, basil, and cilantro fresh for 5–7 days, trim off the stem ends from the bunch, remove any yellowed leaves, and immerse the stems in a container of water, like a bouquet of flowers. Drape a plastic bag loosely over the leaves, secure with a rubber band around the container, and refrigerate.

Dried herbs lose their flavor over time and should be replaced every 6 months or so.

PREPARING HERBS

Remove leaves and sprigs as needed to create or garnish a salad. The leaves of herbs should be removed from the stems before chopping or mincing. Chopping and mincing are easier when the herbs are dry; otherwise, they stick to the knife. Like lettuce leaves, herbs may also be stacked, rolled, and cut crosswise to make shreds, called julienne or chiffonade.

When using dried herbs, crush and roll them between your fingers just before adding them to a dish. This releases their flavorful oils.

USING FRUITS AND VEGETABLES

The recipes in this book assume that fruits and vegetables are carefully washed before use, and each gives instructions on peeling, seeding, and other preparation as needed.

Some fruits and vegetables turn an unappetizing shade of brown once their flesh is cut and exposed to the air. To slow this discoloring, rub or drizzle the cut surfaces with an acid such as lemon juice or a little white vinegar. Or, drop the cut items into a bowl of acidulated water, that is, water mixed with a little acid (see page 37).

These common salad fruits and vegetables discolor on slicing and exposure to air: apples, artichokes, avocados, bananas, cauliflower, celery root (celeriac), eggplants (aubergines), mushrooms, nectarines, parsnips, peaches, pears, and potatoes.

USING CHEESE

To ensure the fullest flavor, bring cheeses to room temperature before serving. Dry-aged cheeses such as Parmesan may be grated on the smallest rasps of a combination grater-shredder. Or, use a vegetable peeler or knife to make shavings.

A semisoft cheese such as Cheddar might be shredded on the larger holes of a grater-shredder, or cut into small cubes. Feta and drier blue cheeses such as Roquefort have a perfect consistency for crumbling, while creamy young goat cheese or Gorgonzola can be scooped up with a spoon and dolloped on a salad.

MAKING SALAD DRESSING

For instructions on making salad dressing, see page 111.

TOSSING A SALAD

When tossing a salad with a dressing, use a light hand. With a pair of salad servers or two large spoons or forks, gently mix the greens or the other vegetables with a relatively small amount of dressing, distributing it with numerous tossings. Do not drench the greens. Dress salad greens just before serving to keep them fresh and crisp, and add garnishes such as toasted nuts at the last minute so that they do not become soggy.

TOASTING NUTS AND SEEDS

Toasting nuts and seeds brings out their richness and gives them a crunch as well as a golden color. Untoasted, they have a more subtle taste and a softer texture. Like herbs, nuts and seeds can be added as a garnish to almost any salad. Sprinkling a table-spoon or 2 across the top just before serving adds not only taste but also style to the finished dish.

HOW TO TOAST NUTS

Preheat the oven to 325°F (165°C). Spread the nuts in a single layer on a baking sheet.

Place the baking sheet in the oven and toast, stirring occasionally, until the nuts are lightly browned, fragrant, and coated in a layer of their own oil. Depending on the type of nut and the size of the pieces, this may take from 10–20 minutes.

Remove the nuts from the pan as soon as they start to look done, pour them onto a plate, and let cool. The nuts will continue to cook slightly after removal from the pan.

Note: Nuts may also be toasted in a small, dry frying pan over medium heat. Shake the pan often, and remove the nuts as soon as they start to brown. Seeds may be toasted in the same way, but watch them very carefully or they may burn.

MAKING DRESSING

Salad dressings fall into two general categories: vinaigrettes and creamy dressings often based on mayonnaise. Both vinaigrettes and mayonnaise involve making an emulsion, or thoroughly blending together two ingredients that normally don't mix, such as oil and vinegar.

Making a stable emulsion, one that will for last more than a few minutes, requires vigorous whisking as well as an agent known as an emulsifier to help hold the other ingredients together. Mustard, for example, is used in many vinaigrettes not just for its flavor, but also for its emulsifying properties. Egg is used as an emulsifier when mixing oil with vinegar or lemon juice to make mayonnaise. Shown opposite are the basic stages in making an emulsion, using mayonnaise as an example:

1 **Mixing egg yolk and salt**: The salt is dissolved into a liquid at the start.

2 **Adding the olive oil**: The oil is poured in very slowly at first, with constant whisking.

3 **The mixture starts to thicken**: The oil may now be added more quickly and the other element of the emulsion (lemon juice) whisked in.

4 **The finished mayonnaise**: The vigorous whisking and the emulsifier (egg) create a stable emulsion.

BASIC VINAIGRETTE

1 tablespoon red wine vinegar

Coarse sea salt

1 teaspoon Dijon mustard (optional)

3 tablespoons extra-virgin olive oil, grapeseed oil, or canola oil

Freshly ground pepper

Put the vinegar and ½ teaspoon salt in a bowl and stir with a fork to dissolve the salt. With the fork, whisk in the mustard. Slowly pour the oil into the vinegar in a thin stream while whisking with the fork. Season with ¼ teaspoon pepper. Makes about 6 tablespoons (3 fl oz/90 ml).

Variation Tip: This vinaigrette combines vinegar and oil in a ratio of 1 part vinegar to 3 parts oil. Other classic proportions are 1 part vinegar to 4 parts oil or to 5 parts oil. Experiment to find a combination you like, or try different oils, vinegars, herbs, and spices. Minced garlic and minced fresh oregano or thyme will give this vinaigrette a Mediterranean flavor. Or, substitute balsamic vinegar for the red wine vinegar for a more aromatic dressing.

BASIC MAYONNAISE

1 egg yolk

Salt

⅔ cup (5 fl oz/160 ml) extra-virgin olive oil, grapeseed oil, or canola oil

1 teaspoon fresh lemon juice

In a bowl, whisk together the egg yolk and 1 teaspoon salt until blended. While whisking, slowly add the oil in a very thin stream, just a little at a time, blending it thoroughly into the egg yolk.

As the mixture begins to thicken, the oil can be added a little more quickly, but don't rush it, or the mayonnaise will separate. Continue until all the oil is used and the mayonnaise is thick.

Whisk in the lemon juice. Refrigerate for up to 2 hours before using. Makes about ⅔ cup (5 fl oz/160 ml).

Note: This recipe contains raw egg. For more information, see page 114.

GLOSSARY

ALMONDS With their delicate flavor and smooth texture, almonds make an elegant garnish or salad ingredient. To blanch, or peel, almonds, place the shelled nuts in a large heatproof bowl and pour boiling water over them. Let stand for about 1 minute, then drain the nuts in a colander and rinse with cold running water to cool. Pinch each nut to slip off its bitter skin.

For instructions on toasting nuts, see page 109.

AVOCADOS To ripen avocados, store them in a warm, dark place for a few days. To speed the ripening process, put the avocado in a paper bag with an apple, a banana, or a tomato. Ethylene gases emitted by the other fruit will hasten ripening.

To pit and peel an avocado, use a small, sharp knife to carefully cut it in half lengthwise around the large, round pit at the center. Rotate the halves in opposite directions to separate them, then remove the pit with the tip of a spoon and discard. Ease a large spoon between the avocado flesh and the peel and gently scoop out the flesh.

BELL PEPPERS (CAPSICUMS), PEELING Using tongs or a large fork, hold the whole peppers, one at a time, over the flame of a gas burner, turning as needed, until the skin is blistered and charred black on all sides, 10–15 minutes. (This may also be done in the broiler [grill], but watch the peppers carefully to avoid burning their flesh.)

Once the skin is blackened and puffy, transfer the peppers to a paper bag and close loosely. This allows the peppers to steam as they cool and helps the skins to loosen. When cool, peel or rub away the charred skin. Do not worry if a little stays on the flesh. Don't rinse the peppers under running water, or you will wash away some flavor.

Lay the peppers on a cutting board. Using a small, sharp knife, slit each pepper lengthwise. Some liquid will run out, so have a bowl ready to catch the juices or mop them up with paper towels. Open the pepper and spread it on the cutting board. Cut around the stem end, then remove the stem, seeds, and white membranes, or ribs. Now slice or dice the pepper according to the instructions in a recipe. If desired, use the juices in the dressing for extra bell-pepper flavor.

BELL PEPPERS (CAPSICUMS), SEEDING Cut the peppers in half crosswise or lengthwise and, using your hands or a knife, remove the stem along with the cluster of seeds. Trim away the remaining seeds and white membranes, or ribs, and cut the pepper to the size and shape indicated in a recipe.

BLUE CHEESES Some cheeses are inoculated with the spores of special molds to develop a fine network of blue veins for a strong, sharp, peppery flavor that intensifies with age. Depending on its texture, blue cheese may be crumbled, diced, spread, or sliced for use in a salad. Some of the most popular types include milder Gorgonzola and Maytag, and stronger Roquefort and Stilton.

CHERVIL A springtime herb with curly, dark green leaves. Best when used fresh in salads, with vegetables, or with eggs, it has mild flavor reminiscent of parsley and anise.

CITRUS REAMER A handheld or free-standing tool designed to squeeze the juice from lemons, usually by means of a mound-shaped ridged surface pressed and twisted against and into a lemon half.

DEGLAZING Using liquid to dislodge and dissolve the browned bits of meat, poultry, or other sautéed or fried food that become stuck to the pan bottom as a result of cooking. The liquid, usually wine, stock, or water, is added to the pan after the food has been removed. The liquid is heated over medium-high or high heat, and the cook stirs it with a wooden spoon or spatula and scrapes the pan bottom at the same time to free the browned bits. The flavorful liquid is reduced, letting it partially cook away or evaporate. The resulting sauce is called a reduction sauce or pan sauce.

DOUBLE BOILER A set of two pans, one nested atop the other with room for water to simmer in the lower pan. Delicate foods and cream sauces are placed in the top pan to heat them gently. Double boilers are also a good place to keep foods warm without cooking them further, at least not too quickly. The top pan should not touch the water beneath, and the water should not boil.

EGG, RAW Eggs are sometimes used raw in dressings and other preparations. Raw eggs run a risk of being infected with salmonella or other bacteria, which can lead to food poisoning. This risk is of most concern to small children, older people, pregnant women, and anyone with a compromised immune system. If you have health and safety concerns, do not consume raw egg, or seek out a pasteurized egg product to replace it. Eggs can also be made safe by heating them to a temperature of 160°F (71°C). Note that coddled, poached, and soft-boiled eggs do not reach this temperature.

EMULSION An emulsion is a mixture of ingredients that would ordinarily not combine, such as oil and vinegar. For more information, see page 111.

GARLIC PRESS This tool makes quick work of mincing peeled garlic cloves. A garlic press is hinged and fitted with a perforated hopper and a plunger that squeezes the garlic through the holes so that it can be mixed more easily with other ingredients. Choose a press that feels comfortable in the hand and has a sturdy, durable hinge.

HARICOTS VERTS Small, slender green beans that are favored in France. Delicately flavored, they are more elegant than other green beans and are also referred to as French green beans or filet beans. Young, slender Blue Lake or other green beans may be substituted.

JULIENNING Cutting food into long, thin matchstick strips called julienne. To julienne a vegetable such as a carrot, first cut the carrot into pieces of a desired length. Cut the pieces into strips, then stack the strips and slice them again to julienne them.

To julienne an herb such as basil, stack several leaves one on top of the other, roll up the stacked leaves length-wise, and slice them crosswise into thin strips. The strips are called a chiffonade. Lettuce and other greens may also be stacked and sliced.

MANGOES, PEELING Always peel mangoes before serving. Slit the thick, sometimes leathery skin with a knife tip and pull it off in strips.

To cut a mango, first peel it with a knife, and then stand the mango on one of its narrow edges, the stem end point-ing toward you. With a large, sharp knife, cut down about 1 inch (2.5 cm) to one side of the stem, just grazing the side of the pit. Repeat with the other side of the fruit. Place the mango pieces cut side down on a cutting board and slice as needed. If desired, trim the remaining flesh from the pit as well.

MAYONNAISE This mixture of vinegar or lemon juice, oil, and egg has become a common household condiment. But if you've never made and used home-made mayonnaise in a recipe, it will be a revelation. It may be done in a food processor, but a small amount is easily made by hand. See page 111.

OLIVE OIL "Extra-virgin" is a term applied to the highest grade of olive oil, which is extracted from the fruit without the use of heat or chemicals. It has a clear, greenish brown hue and a fine, fruity, sometimes slightly peppery flavor. Its rich color and fruity fragrance and taste make it the preferred choice for salad dressings and marinades.

PANCETTA This flavorful Italian bacon is made by rubbing a slab of pork belly with a mix of spices that may include cinnamon, cloves, or juniper. The slab is rolled into a tight cylinder and cured for at least 2 months. Because it is not smoked, pancetta is more moist and silky than regular bacon.

PROSCIUTTO Neither smoked nor cooked, prosciutto is Italian ham that is the seasoned, salt-cured, air-dried rear leg of pork. The best-known prosciutto comes from Parma in the Italian region of Emilia-Romagna, where it is aged from 10 months to 2 years. It is called prosciutto di Parma and is labeled with a five-pointed star seared into its side. Best when served raw or lightly cooked, its slightly salty flavor is a traditional accompaniment to sweet fresh fruits and melons.

ROMAINE, HEARTS OF The pale and crunchy inner leaves of a head of romaine (cos) lettuce, referred to as the heart, are often favored for salads.

SALAD SPINNER Consisting of a lidded container with an inner colander-like basket, a salad spinner makes short work of drying lettuce and other greens, preventing the salad dressing from becoming too watery.

SALMON, SMOKED Rich in texture and sweet in flavor, smoked salmon is a delicacy. There are two primary methods for smoking salmon. Hot-smoked salmon is smoked for 6–12 hours at a temperature of 120°–180°F (49°–82°C). This method also cooks the salmon and ultimately yields a flaky texture. Cold-smoked salmon is smoked anywhere from 1 day to 3 weeks at a temperature of 70°–90°F (21°–32°C) and results in a silken texture. Most recipes use cold-smoked salmon, which is available freshly sliced in delicatessens, specialty-food stores, and well-stocked markets.

SEA SALT Created by natural evapora-tion, sea salt is available in coarse or fine grains that are shaped like hollow, flaky pyramids. Due to its shape, it adheres better to foods and dissolves more

quickly than table salt. It also has more flavor than table salt, and smaller amounts should be used to season foods. Stores carry sea salt primarily from France, England, and the United States. The most prized is the grayish-ivory Fleur du Sel from Brittany.

SERRANO CHILES Serranos are similar to jalapeños in heat intensity, but the serrano is sleeker in shape and has a distinctly sharp taste. About 2 inches (5 cm) long, serranos may be green or red. Most often, they are used fresh.

TOMATOES, PEELING AND SEEDING To peel and seed tomatoes, bring a large saucepan three-fourths full of water to a boil. Using a sharp knife, cut a shallow X in the blossom end of each tomato. Immerse the tomatoes in the boiling water for 15–30 seconds, then, using a slotted spoon, remove and transfer them to a work surface. When cool enough to handle, slip off the skins. To seed, slice the tomatoes in half crosswise. Hold each half over a sink or bowl and lightly squeeze and shake it to dislodge the seeds, using your finger if needed to help ease them out.

TUNA, CANNED When shopping for canned tuna, look for oil-packed tuna for the best flavor. If you can find an Italian brand of oil-packed tuna, choose it. Italian canned tuna is often pink meat, from the belly of the fish, which is moister than the more widely available white-meat tuna. If you cannot find tuna

packed in olive oil, buy water-packed tuna, drain it, put it in extra-virgin olive oil, cover, and refrigerate for 2 or 3 days before using.

VINAIGRETTE The simplest, best-known form of salad dressing is a vinaigrette, a term that takes its name from vinegar but has broadened to describe any blend of vinegar or lemon juice with oil. See page 111.

INDEX

118

APPLE PRESS
Sheridan House, 4th Floor
112-116A Western Road
Hove , East Sussex BN3 1DD
United Kingdom

WELDON OWEN INC.
Chief Executive Officer: John Owen
President: Terry Newell
Chief Operating Officer: Larry Partington
Vice President, International Sales: Stuart Laurence
Creative Director: Gaye Allen
Series Editor: Sarah Putman Clegg
Associate Editor: Heather Belt
Production Manager: Chris Hemesath
Production Assistant: Donita Boles
Studio Manager: Brynn Breuner
Photograph Editor: Lisa Lee

A Weldon Owen Production
Copyright © 2001 by Weldon Owen Inc. and
Williams-Sonoma Inc.

First Apple Press edition printed in 2002.

ISBN 1 84092 351 2

10 9 8 7 6 5 4 3 2 1

Set in Trajan, Utopia, and Vectora.

CColor separations by Bright Arts Graphics
Singapore (Pte.) Ltd.
Printed and bound in Singapore by Tien Wah
Press (Pte.) Ltd.

A NOTE ON WEIGHTS AND MEASURES

All recipes include customary U.S. and metric measurements. Metric conversions are based on
a standard developed for these books and have been rounded off. Actual weights may vary.